DECOLONIZE DRAG

T0036662

Also from *Decolonize That! Handbooks for the Revolutionary Overthrow of Embedded Colonial Ideas*

Edited by Bhakti Shringarpure

DECOLONIZE DRAG

KAREEM KHUBCHANDANI

OR Books
New York · London

The *Decolonize That!* series is produced by OR Books in collaboration with Warscapes magazine.

© 2023 Kareem Khubchandani

Published by OR Books, New York and London

Visit our website at www.orbooks.com

All rights information: rights@orbooks.com

First printing 2023

Cataloging-in-Publication data is available from the Library of Congress.
A catalog record for this book is available from the British Library.

Typeset by Lapiz Digital Services. Printed by BookMobile, USA, and CPI, UK.

paperback ISBN 978-1-68219-395-2 • ebook ISBN 978-1-68219-396-9

CONTENTS

EDITOR'S PREFACE

BHAKTI SHRINGARPURE

It is a strange twist in the tale that a radical, dissident, beautifully amorphous and sometimes clandestine art form such as drag has today become an empire racking up millions. The legendary RuPaul, creator, host and rainmaker of the reality show *RuPaul's Drag Race* might immediately come to mind. But think also of Trixie Mattel, or Alyssa Edwards, or Bianca Del Rio, who have amassed equal millions of Instagram followers as their dollar net worths. Empire begets empire and that they all emerged as power players because of RuPaul's music, performance and drag conglomerate is proof of this. Though it can be a default moralizing mode to turn up our noses at this grubby game of cash, caché and celebrity mongering, it is hard to begrudge drag artists their success and to not view them through a lens of courage. Drag has an inherent capacity to evoke pleasure, politics, physical rigor, and awe. Even passively consuming an unabashedly gender-bending drag performance can feel rebellious, since we still live in a conservative and normative world where gender binarism, hetero-patriarchy, queerphobia and sexism remain firmly entrenched.

But what if drag's rise to the top of its game as a popular, commercial art form has meant selling out and feeding right into problematic gender binaries, whiteness, or coloniality? Once you start indulging these suspicions, you're sure to find plenty of RuPaul quotes that might soothe. Like this one: "All sins are forgiven once you start making a lot of money." Or: "The key to navigating this life—don't take it too seriously. That's when the party begins." While these might seem like vulgar declarations, RuPaul and the mainstream drag world can get away with them because they are anchored in the idea that drag is subversive at its core. So if it is now being beamed into everyone's screens and broadening our minds and making us woke, why should we start churning with all this empire talk? Why overthink? Why spoil the party? Come on now, it only just began.

Well, stop right there, because scholar Kareem Khubchandani and his fabulous drag avatar LaWhore Vagistan do not want us to buy into these false logics. The duo is here to answer the age-old existential question: if it feels so right, why is it wrong?

Decolonize Drag by Kareem and drag aunty LaWhore is a paradigm-shifting meditation on drag's extraordinary power and its simultaneous cooptation by market forces today. This unique book successfully dismantles the thickly entwined bulwark of race, gender, class, and ability through a meditation on a form of expression which has a presence and a history almost everywhere in the world. *Decolonize Drag* starts on a somber note, as LaWhore tells the story of finding herself in Texas during the protests in the wake of Freddie Gray's death in cop custody in Baltimore. LaWhore and the other drag queens are reminded of the Stonewall riots in 1969, when LGBTQ protesters had risen up against the police, and in which queer and trans Black and Brown people had played an instrumental part. LaWhore realizes that this urgency and these histories of brutal criminalization of "bodies, genders, and desires" have come to be largely forgotten in the blur of corporate-sponsored drag parades and Pride months.

Disappointed with the turn that drag has taken today, LaWhore asks: "What would drag look like if it was not in subservience to and collusion with colonial aesthetic and knowledge forms?" To answer LaWhore's poignant questions, we are handed over to Kareem, brilliant scholar and patient teacher who holds our hand through a history of drag from below. Kareem returns us to the insurgent and anticolonial core of drag, and and rescues it from its present-day whiteness, gender binarism, and profit imperatives.

The five chapters of *Decolonize Drag* are an eye-opening adventure, and Kareem's talent for juggling the roles of teacher, scholar, and performer means that we are learning, we are critiquing, we are dismantling—but we are also intimately placed alongside transgressor figures whose bodies bear the scars of cruel colonial histories. Drag today has been "occupied." Popular culture insists that drag is just queens and kings (usually queens, really) who produce glamorous spectacles usually through heavily feminized aesthetics like big hair, high heels and perfect lip syncing. Drag as it is represented and experienced by audiences today tends to focus on the performance of crossing and transgressing gender. Kareem reminds us that "gender is *not* the only or primary identity or politic being staged; race, nation, language, religion are all salient parts of drag, as are the multitude of visual, literary, and media references cited by performers in their music, dress, movement, and makeup." And this is where colonialism comes into the mix and, more importantly, the ways in which gender works as a "colonial tool." Topics such as which races are more effeminate or which ones have higher sexual appetites or who can dance or sing better still remain completely normalized in media, in research and in casual conversations. Kareem connects the dots to show that empire's civilizing missions, with its strategic and violent use of science and culture have generated these pernicious binaries of sex, race and gender.

Conquest, Kareem writes, "compels the colonizer to put on display their imagined version of the sexual and gender perversity of the racialized Other." This book proves just how urgently we need a decolonized drag to break, bust, shatter, unsettle and undo the binary structures put in place by Euro-American empires. *Decolonize Drag* also exposes the ways in which neoliberal regimes beget hyper-professionalization which in the drag universe leads to overly curated looks and choreography; in short, a push towards perfection. The final chapter, "Just Do It! Techniques and Technologies for Decolonizing Drag" explicitly counters this trend. Kareem offers a how-to guide for decolonized, messy, fucked-up, untidy, de-professionalized and emancipated drag.

Much like the topic it tackles, the book functions on many different levels. There's the critical-thinking part and there's the deliberate-unlearning part, but the most delightful aspect of the book is the "doing" part. So, don't let the shiny cover fool you. In encouraging readers to create this new world through their bodies, Kareem not only expands the meaning of drag but paves the way for what decolonizing itself might mean.

INTRODUCTION

Hai!

It's me, LaWhore Vagistan, your favorite, over-educated, over-opinionated, over-dressed, South Asian drag aunty. I'm glad you're reading this little book. Kareem didn't think he could tell the story alone and wanted a famous voice from the drag world to be part of the story. He couldn't afford one, so he asked me. Ha! Aunty is here to give you some perspective from an actual drag artist, not just a stressed-out scholar. Are we ready to spill the chai?

Picture it: Austin, Texas, 2015. It's six in the evening at a dive bar on Red River Street, and ten drag queens are gathered around a high-top table. The manager is telling us: "Pick up your own tips. No stealing. Watch your stuff. Make sure you give the DJ your music." It's opening night of the inaugural Austin International Drag Festival, a first-of-its-kind event featuring drag artists, vendors, headliners, and opportunities for amateurs. The city was overrun by drag! Drag festivals like Wigstock (est. 1984) and Bushwig (est. 2012) in New York City certainly preceded Austin's Festival, but girl, Austin has mastered the festival format. Like SXSW and Austin City Limits, this drag festival was massive in scope. Every downtown bar, gay and straight, had a drag show scheduled. The mornings featured marketplaces selling wigs, zines, binders, and jewelry. The afternoons showcased panels, workshops, and live recordings of queer podcasts. And at night there were drag artists serving every gender, species, and object you could fathom.

We're only half in drag. It's Texas in May, and so way too hot to be in full lewks before the sun has fully set. TBQH I'm not sure why they asked us to get here so early. I guess they're nervous about everything since this was the festival's launch. And because queens are always late! Amiright? The event manager runs through the performance set; we're each supposed to perform two numbers, though there's no designated changing area. Typical!

Suddenly we can't hear ourselves talking. "Black Lives!" "Matter!" "Black Lives!" "Matter!" "No justice!" "No peace!" "No justice!" "No peace!" A little over two weeks prior, a twenty-five-year-old Black man named Freddie Gray died while in the custody of the Baltimore Police, due to the use of excessive force during his arrest. In the wake of his death, Black Lives Matter protests erupted across the US protesting extrajudicial violence against Black people. Austin's protesters march past our venue, drowning out our pedantic planning. We stop talking, trying to figure out what the commotion is. One queen—she's not white, but I'm not sure of her race either, queens of color need that lightening makeup for the stage, you know? She says, to break the ice and get us back to work: "Ignore them. That has nothing to do with us."

A pregnant silence tells us that we don't fully agree. "That has *everything* to do with us," I say. I really don't have to say more. Our silence says we understand. That moment forced us to reflect on the Black and Brown drag queens, cross-dressers, gender rebels, and sex workers who were central to sparking the 1969 Stonewall Riots in New York, riots against the harassment of LGBTQ people *by* the police. We commemorate Stonewall and other uprisings like it with annual global Pride celebrations. But decades of fanfare and flair at Pride have diluted the urgency of that sticky Sunday in June 1969 when queer patrons of the Stonewall Inn resisted police harassment. Instead we drag queens sit pretty in corporate-funded floats, waving graciously at happy faces who have forgotten that our bodies, genders, and desires were once criminalized.

In 2020, protests in the wake of the murder of George Floyd by Minneapolis Police coincided with

Pride month. While Pride festivities were anyways subdued due to the COVID-19 pandemic that kept much of the world indoors, the mainstream narrative around Pride pivoted from boas, glitter, and corporate parade floats to "The Stonewall riots were a protest against police violence." Op-eds and blogs uplifted the roles of Marsha P. Johnson and Sylvia Rivera in the Stonewall uprisings and their radical organizing for trans rights and safety in the wake of the protests. Johnson and Rivera were Black and Latina activists who variously described themselves as gay, transgender, and drag queens. As the Black Lives Matter protestors chanted past our bar, my fellow drag queens and I paused to remember that our right to glamor, pleasure, and safety rested on the blows and shouts and organizing strategies of Marsha and Sylvia and their queer and trans kin. And not just theirs; so many queer and trans figures paved the way for the transformative possibilities we enjoy in the drag world.

The safety of trans, nonbinary, and gender-nonconforming people remains far from secure. As protests burgeoned during Pride month 2020, Black queer and trans people continued to be killed; that June alone Dominique "Rem'mie" Fells, Riah Milton, Brayla Stone, and Merci Mack were murdered.

I don't have a pretty follow-up for you. We got silent, and then awkward, and then moved on. Sorry, girl. Our fabulosity and feathers often make it easy to forget the histories of violence and activism that preceded our show—laws against cross-dressing, police harassment, protests, vigils, and die-ins. But for that very reason, our show offered a momentary respite from engaging the ongoing violence around us in Texas at that time: the rapid gentrification in Austin displacing Black and Latinx longtime residents, the not-so-distant dehumanizing detainment at the US-Mexico border, the perpetual violence against Black and trans folks, and the extractive economies centered around oil production. And of course, since the sixteenth century, Texas has been subject to French, Spanish, and Anglo-American colonization decimating and displacing Native people. It's 2023 as I write this and lawmakers in the US are *still* criminalizing drag, denying healthcare to people based on gender and sex, and punishing teachers for talking about LGBTQ issues in the classroom.

The Austin International Drag Festival and others like it that celebrate dissident genders and desires provide an alternative to the ongoing crises around us. It was a feel-good weekend filled with virtuosic performances by Black, Asian, Latinx, and Indigenous gender rebels, monsters, and unicorns. The joy and community-making that drag affords are life-sustaining in an ever-violent world! And particularly in a conservative state like Texas! The grassroots nature of this first-of-its-kind festival felt sweet and full of possibility. But it was overshadowed with the announcement, just weeks prior to the festival, that entertainment mogul RuPaul Charles, with production company World of Wonder, would host the first ever RuPaul's DragCon in the Fall. Austin's scrappy grassroots festival suddenly felt small in the face of the celebrities announced at DragCon.

Black drag queen RuPaul, whose punk androgynous style from the eighties has transformed into corporate Glamazon over more than thirty years, looms large in the global story of drag. Her rise to fame through her super-successful reality TV competition *RuPaul's Drag Race* and its many spinoffs has catapulted drag out of its subcultural spaces in nightclubs, cabarets, and festivals and into mainstream media. Hundreds of drag queens are now household names worldwide thanks to the show. But RuPaul and her network producers have distilled drag into a very limited form of gender performance. My hairy-chested drag would never cut it on the show. Only recently has the show welcomed trans women, trans men, cis women, and nonbinary people, though it still doesn't include drag kings. *RuPaul's Drag Race* has cast a shadow over the magnificent possibilities of performance we could call drag, foreclosing access to drag, fame, money, representation, mobility, and legibility to so many! These days, drag has to emulate what we see on *Drag Race* and at DragCon to be understood *as* drag. The empire she's built extracts from and controls smaller pockets of creativity.

But what if drag remembered its histories of dissidence? What if drag had permission to move across categories and media? What worlds, more just and beautiful worlds, could drag make possible if it didn't solely look like what RuPaul and her production team put out? What would drag look like if it was not in subservience to and in collusion with colonial aesthetics and knowledge forms? And can we perform decolonial critiques through drag without losing the fun, play, and pleasure drag is known for?

Oof! Those are big questions to answer, and I have a show to do, so I'll let The Professor take it from here. Happy reading!

Ex. Oh. Ex.
—Aunty

1. LaWhore Vagistan in her signature sari, precariously perched on a spiral stair, because she'll do anything to get the photo! Photo by Mettie Ostrowski.

2. KaMani Sutra poses in her South Asian finery, decorated also with her beard and body hair. Photo by Maz V-Talukdar.

3. Femme queens at the judges table compete in a realness category. From Gerard Gaskin's series *Legendary*, photographed at the Coldest Winter Ever Ball, Jan 30, 2016. Photo by Gerard Gaskin.

4. Merrie Cherry, based in Brooklyn, prepares to film a live-stream drag show in April 2020 during COVID-19-related shutdowns. Photo by Santiago Felipe/Getty Images.

5. "RuPaul With Grass Skirt" (1987). This image captures an early incarnation of RuPaul that drew from punk as much as pageantry. Photo by Al Clayton Photography, LLC/Getty Images.

6. Ilona Verley (from Skuppah, Nlaka'pamux descent) poses barefoot wearing an outfit with ribbons and jingles that signal their Indigenous heritage. Their red-gloved gesture shows solidarity with the Missing and Murdered Indigenous Women movement. Situated in this natural environment, they also invoke First Nations people's connection to the land and water. Photo by Fernando Cysneiros.

7. Papi Churro, using skulls, feathers, gold, and blue, stages his Mayan and Aztec ancestry while also performing queer punk. Photo by Devlin Shand.

8. Kristy Yummykochi in "Never Again is Now" from the Rice Rockettes BIG 10-year anniversary show. Instead of backup dancers that usually help drag queens with costume changes, the accompanying "hot boys" in Kristi's performance are dressed as ICE officers who aggressively disrobe her. Image courtesy of the artist.

9. Faluda Islam in zombie-inspired drag, repping their religious and national histories with moon and star pasties on their chest. Photo by Humayun Memon.

10. Miss Toto as Harriet Tubman, in a still from a web-based video performance. In the video we see Tubman/Toto running through actual fields and rivers in search of freedom.

Chapter 1

HAIRY SITUATIONS: DRAG, PERFORMANCE, AND GENDER BINARIES

In 2014, I sent undergraduate students in my "Queer Of Color Performance" class at Northwestern University to watch the drag show at a queer Bollywood party in Chicago called *Jai Ho!* In the city's predominantly white gay nightlife scene, this quarterly fundraiser promised an inclusive space for South Asians and other people of color, and celebrated music and film from South Asia and its diasporas. Headlining this night was none other than your favorite aunty, LaWhore Vagistan, along with several other queer and trans South Asian artists. Nightlife and drag shows have an important legacy as venues of community-making for historically marginalized people. They also have important material consequences, such as raising money for HIV/AIDS care and education[1] and funding scholarships for Indigenous youth.[2]

Reporting back on the show, one white student told me that when he started to clap for LaWhore at the end of her performance, another white party patron interrupted his applause, putting his hands over my student's: "Don't clap for them. They're not real drag queens." This older man felt the need to educate my student on what kind of drag one should appreciate, inviting him into an implicit system of value of what counts as drag. We don't know if the man didn't like the performances because they were by novice drag artists, because the queens lip-synched to Bollywood songs instead of the usual US diva canon, because some of the drag queens didn't wear any makeup or were hairy-chested, or because the performances were poorly executed by his standards. Whatever his measure, he felt the authority to question the authenticity of our drag: "They're not real drag queens." I was *shook*! My face burned from imposter syndrome, from anger that this white man could come into our nightlife sanctuary and dismiss our creativity and fun as "not real drag."

This is the crux of *Decolonize Drag*—that the category of performance we call drag has been occupied by particular forms of whiteness (binary gender, professionalism, disaffected irony) that regulate and deny access to the genre for many, particularly people of color and Indigenous people from across the globe, as well as poor and disabled artists. While drag is known for its transgressive nature, the flattening of the form forgets that gender dissidence necessarily looks different depending on social, cultural, and historical context. This book explores "drag" as a category, asking how it can be capacious of more kinds of performers and artistry. Though drag has acquired so much cultural capital in the last decade, it is confined to a select cadre of artists. Rethinking the categories, aesthetics, and locations of drag has the potential to redistribute wealth, attention, politics, and beauty. If there was greater variety under the drag umbrella, we would see artists speak back to oppressive forms of authority, we would witness aesthetics that undo the binds of coloniality.

Popular culture, movies like *To Wong Foo, Thanks for Everything! Julie Newmar*, *The Birdcage*, and *Priscilla, Queen of the Desert* have given us a dominant globalized image of drag. We usually imagine a drag queen, specifically a cisgender gay man styled in glamorous feminine attire (perhaps a gown, maybe a cocktail dress), sparkling makeup, hair that reaches for the heavens, and stilettos, lip-synching to a disco song. This queen's novelty derives from her ability to produce a spectacle, be it her sequin gown and hair teased high or her unexpectedly tall and muscular frame. This ubiquitous vision of drag suggests that binary gender crossings—men impersonating women and women masquerading as men—are the primary measure of the performer's excellence and the premiere pleasure of the audience's interest.

One of the problems with this generalized, commercial drag queen figure is that she does not exemplify the diversity of drag in the US, nor across the globe. For one, there are more categories than kings and queens. But even the category of "queen" includes cisgender *and* transgender women performing in highly feminized aesthetics—no gender "crossing" occurs, at least not a prescriptively binary one. For many drag audiences, the pleasure they take in performance comes less from the fantasies of crossing gender, and more from the *invention of gender* and the *creation of alternative worlds.* Also, gender is *not* the only or primary identity or politic being staged; race, nation, language, religion are all salient parts of drag, as are the multitude of visual, literary, and media references cited by performers in their music, dress, movement, and makeup.

Processes of colonization, as I demonstrate across Chapter 1 and 2, have often confirmed racial difference *through* gender, so the performance of gender can never be the sole axis through which we make sense of drag. A decolonial approach to drag focuses on the multiple ways gender is co-constituted by race, migration, class, and disability, and the potential for audiences and performers to explore these issues through the ribald and playful performance genre. I understand decolonization not as a return to forms of gender lost to colonial discipline and erasure, but rather the imperative to invent other styles, aesthetics, and ways of being in our bodies in the wake of loss and toward more beautiful futures.

If coloniality is a project of dispossession, extraction, and privatization, decolonial drag must imagine itself as abundant, available, and accessible. There are many ways that drag has been coopted into reifying and naturalizing normative gender roles, and uplifting styles associated with the most privileged stratas of societies. This leaves those of us who don't do gender the same way, or don't do it "well," feeling like imposters, alien to the category of human, let alone to the world of drag. To decolonize drag requires mapping how gender works as a colonial tool, in order to undo, avoid, divert, and subvert these projects. In addition to rethinking "drag" as a performance of gender crossing, it requires saying yes to performers that don't look like "real drag queens." It requires a more capacious mind and generous heart that witnesses performance not for the perfection of executing gender, but celebrates the shared worlds that performers conjure for their audiences through the body.

People often ask me for the history of drag as an art form, but that's not really the scope of this project; in fact, I'm trying to undo the often singular and linear mindsets around what we think of as drag, which makes a history hard to write. Let me mention that my favorite texts thinking about drag in both an historical and global frame are Laurence Senelick's *The Changing Room*, Sasha Velour's *The Big Reveal*, and Jake Hall's *The Art of Drag*. My hope is that across this book, you learn to see drag through a multifaceted eyeglass that holds numerous artistic practices and gender categories in your view at once. To decolonize drag, I'm suggesting that we decenter gender as the sole rubric of evaluating the practice—this requires understanding that gender is simultaneously constituted by race, religion, class, ability, and more.

However, it would be unfair to you to proceed without at least a loose definition of drag. Here's my take: drag is a genre of performance practiced in entertainment, nightlife, and festival contexts by and/or for gender and sexual dissidents—primarily the people who fall under the umbrella categories of queer and transgender, but also many others at the margins of normative gender and sexual configurations. Drag artists exploit the aesthetics of gender in mainstream culture (the poses of sex symbols and models; forms of regional dress and hairstyle; dance moves and gestures replicated from music videos and soap operas) to transform themselves while singing, lip-synching, emceeing, and dancing.

When I say they "exploit" the aesthetics of gender, this can mean marshalling styles and archetypes to their most obvious ends, but it might also mean using and then rejecting them, or perhaps turning them on their heads. Don't worry, there are many examples to come in subsequent chapters.

The style, song, and movement references that drag artists employ are far from arbitrary; they regularly draw on a community's insider knowledge and make artistic choices that they know will spark memories and feelings. As performers occupy the stage or wander through the crowd, they become the night's protagonist: they turn these styles and their meanings into common knowledge, a shared grammar of dissident citizenship.[3] Drawing on these references, drag artists please their audiences by bringing to life, and into proximity, scenes and characters that may only live on screen, in fantasy, or in memory. For the performer, drag is an opportunity to indulge in the temporary fame of the nightclub stage or YouTube screen. Drag is an experimental ground, an opportunity to try on ways of being denied to us by the respectability required in family, work, education settings, in public space. For queer and trans people who don't easily see ourselves—our desires, fantasies, tastes, genders—reflected in the dominant sphere, drag offers opportunities for us to come together and turn imagination into a collective practice.

The drag I love most exists as everyday artistry. I love being able to walk into a bar at 9 p.m. on a Tuesday and in a single show be transported into Greek mythology, whipped around Cardi and Megan's WAP, and then drenched in Prince's purple precipitation. Drag, as I know it, is not hidden behind velvet ropes, it's not conscripted to the bleak galleries of a museum, it's not relegated to distant stages. I'm not breaking the bank to get my life, and it's not a once-in-a-lifetime happening. I love getting to come back the next day, or week, or month, and having my pussoise turned inside-out each time. But not all drag is as easy to access or achieve.

Drag is a global subcultural performance genre associated with gender and sexual rebels, one that retools the most mundane elements of gender like facial hair and hips to bring pleasure and possibility to those who are denied social or state recognition. However, the cultural, artistic, and activist practice that we know as drag has come to be measured through global whiteness—those symbols, styles, gestures, and forms of knowledge we associate with and primarily afford white people. This includes the masculine/feminine binary, professionalism, wealth, choreography (as opposed to improvisation), and geopolitical mobility. This means that certain performances, like LaWhore's at *Jai Ho!* (which was meant to invite in and please South Asian queer people who occupy the margins of this predominantly white Chicago gay bar) fail to *be* drag when they do not sufficiently approximate white ideals. This is precisely what that older man was trying to teach my student when he said, "Don't clap for them"!

Decolonize Drag dismantles the arbitration of this community art form, dethrones a singular authority or aesthetic, in order to (re)open access to drag, to call more things "drag," to reconsider what we think of as "good" drag. Abundance, availability, access. I do so by: thinking through the racialized nature of gender performance (Chapter 2); mapping how drag colludes with white supremacy and global capitalism through the figure of RuPaul Charles and her show *RuPaul's Drag Race* (Chapter 3); documenting drag artists' critiques of colonialism and violence and their invention of alternative worlds (Chapter 4); and offering strategies for us all to engage drag in ways that upend and divest from whiteness and other forms of coloniality (Chapter 5). My familiarity with drag comes from ten years of ethnographic fieldwork in LGBTQ communities in India and the South Asian diaspora; queer partygoing in London,

Toronto, Torremolinos, Bangkok, Dhaka, Mexico City, Bali, Cape Town, San Juan, Manila, Jakarta, and across the US; a decade-long obsession with the *RuPaul's Drag Race* franchise; interdisciplinary scholarship on gender, race and performance; digital recordings of drag performances available online; and my involvement in drag communities as LaWhore Vagistan.

Before we get to the performances, I want to introduce you to some of the terms and foundational ideas that I am relying on to understand relationships between gender, performance, and coloniality.

Gender, Binaries, and Beyond

Drag is much more than men dressing as women and vice versa, and the diversity of drag genres (kings, queens, gender illusion, impersonation, genderfuck, tranimal, etc.) reveals the mutability of sex and gender. If this feels new to you, or even if it doesn't, I want to briefly outline some basics so that we're on the same page. Gender Studies 101, if you will. I want to break down terms like sex and gender, but also build them back up by connecting them to histories of colonization.

Sex is commonly used to refer to the categories by which humans are differentiated based on a variety of biological factors including genitalia, hormone production, chromosomal markers, gamete size, and secondary sex characteristics like breast size, hair growth patterns, and hip width. Usually, at a child's birth or even when viewing a fetus in utero, a doctor will examine the genitalia and assign a male or female sex by saying, "It's a boy," or "It's a girl." On the ultrasound that my hetero couple—I only keep one—have on their fridge, the doctor has written "BOY" right on the child's penis. It's just so extra! These ritual pronouncements have become even more elaborate in the form of "gender reveal" parties, which have notoriously started wildfires on the US West Coast.[4] Such absurd news stories always prompt LaWhore to smugly say, "The gender binary is deadly!" Based on this assignation, children are raised according to a cultural system we know as gender, a constellation of symbols, practices, rituals, and meanings that are reproduced by institutions such as religion, family, healthcare, science, policy, and that binarize everything from pronouns to dress to hobbies to occupation, and so on.

The binary formation of sex is a fiction of human biology and anatomy that papers over the existence of intersex people, people whose biological characteristics vary from the two-category formation. Sex isn't *just* determined by genitalia (see above), but also genitalia

can vary from penis-testes or vagina-ovaries configurations. Sometimes variations may show up at the onset of
puberty, well after a doctor has proclaimed "It's a girl!"
Also, this rigid attachment to a binary has meant that
doctors decide for babies and children with "ambig-
uous" genitalia what sex they should be and perform
nonconsensual surgeries on intersex children based on
an interpretive standard.[5]

The binary sex system that actively buries the existence of intersex people allows us to believe in a binary
gender system, allows us to believe that the cultural
roles of boys/men and girls/women correlate to biological traits. Notions of masculinity and femininity certainly exist across geography and culture, but they aren't
always fixed to sex. Other gender possibilities abound:
muxe, kathoey, lhamana, fa'afafine, travestí, butch queen,
aravani, two-spirit. The ideas that there are *only* two
genders and that sex is prescriptively fixed to gender are
distinctly Euro-western knowledge formations, consol-
idated as recently as the eighteenth century,[6] that reproduce a binary sex/gender system. Through the twentieth
century, clinicians have been central to preserving this
fiction, denying young people, and especially people of
color, the right to define gender on their own terms.[7]
The naturalization of masculinity and femininity in

sexed bodies is a strategy for consolidating power, particularly when it associates cultural meaning and moral-
ity with the body. This might look like the assumption
that only people assigned male and thus occupying the
social category of men are able to make "rational" deci-
sions about statehood, money, and autonomy.

Securing the cultural binary reproduces the biological binary *and* confers power hierarchy onto men. Sex
and gender confirm each other as binaries to stabilize
patriarchal power.

Transgender is used in contemporary cultural contexts to refer to people who do not conform to the gender they were scripted into based on their assigned sex.
This definition of transgender (or trans) is especially
broad. It includes people who transition in ways that
conform to common understandings of masculinity
and femininity, and of male and female bodies, so that
they can move through the world with in accordance
with their own self-perception and hopefully with a
sense of safety, comfort, and pleasure. But it also suggests that people don't necessarily move from female to
male, or from masculine to feminine. Trans people can
be androgynous, nonbinary, gender-nonconforming,
they may have surgeries or hormonal treatments that
modify their sexual characteristics, or they may not.

This might mean that a female-assigned person can perform in visibly feminine ways, and might also be deeply emotionally, spiritually, or aesthetically invested in their femininity, but not identify as a girl or woman or female. This is sometimes referred to as "f2F, or female to Femme transition."[8]

Like sex, gender is constituted not by one designation, but by many cultural protocols: how you cross your legs, groom your body, wear your hair, the volume and speed at which you talk, what clothes you wear, how you understand yourself, how you imagine your spirit. As such, trans people can perform their sex/gender through a variety of means, not just surgery or hormones, but also dress, name, style, or psychic affirmation.[9] And yet, how we identify is always negotiated in relation to the cultural protocols that make us recognizable to others: skirts instead of pants, sneakers instead of heels, flat chests instead of breasts. Shortly, I'll also explain how race is central to making us (and our genders) legible to others.

Gender is a kind of work that we do to present our bodies in the world,[10] but it is also a work that is done when people react, praise, ignore, and grimace in response to what they see.[11] We come to know others' and our own genders through performance, through an actor-audience relationship in which the audience can reflect an image, feeling, or idea that you're putting into the world back to you. The audience could even be you looking at yourself in the mirror or hearing your own voice. This means that gender manifests *between* what we do and how it is interpreted. Even a lack of reaction is its own interpretation, suggesting that something is normal, not disruptive. UK-based Muslim Iraqi drag queen Glamrou writes it so clearly in their memoir:

> One of the things I've come to find interesting about being in drag is that once you're dressed and made up, you so rarely *see* yourself in drag . . . As a result, your image belongs more to the people who are viewing you, and you start to perceive yourself in how you are being perceived in the eyes gazing at you.[12]

What mainstream culture designates as masculine or feminine may feel arbitrary, but through constant repetition—in literature, on TV, in the way bathroom stalls are arranged, in the different clothing sections at a department store—particular things get coded as masculine and others as feminine. Gender is both what we do *and* how we and others see, interpret, and react to that doing. We often cannot point to the origin moments of how symbols and objects become affiliated with gender, and these designations certainly change over time.[13] One way I like to take stock of how such designations shift is following the perpetual public debates over appropriate styles for men—meggings, murses, man buns—that eventually normalize these stylistic choices as gender neutral.

I'm interested in drag's potential to appropriate and unsettle these normative codes. When LaWhore is in drag, she leaves her hairy forearms and chest visibly unshaven even though she might be wearing a heavily embroidered sari or sequined cocktail dress. While this may be jarring to audiences when they first see her— many people expect someone in a sari to be elegantly smooth skinned—by the end of the show these gender contradictions seem to fall away and make room for a different kind of beauty. They fall away because the audience gets used to them and starts to see these incongruences as normal or even gorgeous.

We like to say masculinity and femininity are on a spectrum, suggesting a linear mapping, but queer critic Eve Sedgwick suggests we think of them as being on perpendicular axes instead.[14] Imagine a graph that has femininity on one axis and masculinity on the other. The more elements of femininity you pile onto yourself, that you assemble, the more obviously the world sees you as a woman. As such a person can have masculine traits like short hair and wearing pants, but with noticeable breasts and wide hips they have "enough" femininity apparent to be interpreted as a woman. Sedgwick's threshold model doesn't stage all the complexities of gender, but its multidimensional frame is helpful for a couple of reasons. It helps us imagine the *many* elements that cultivate gender so that we might understand how furry-femme LaWhore Vagistan conjures the effortlessly elegant Bollywood divas she's referencing through facial expression, gesture, song choice, dress, and dance steps, even if she doesn't conform to conventional embodiments of the light-skinned, hairless, skinny Bollywood starlet.

This axis arrangement allows us to imagine people who don't present themselves in ways that read as masculine *or* feminine; we often think of them as androgynous, and they would be very close to the corner where the axes meet. But then there are those who steer quite far away from both axes, who have hulking muscles *and* long hair *and* makeup *and* pointy painted nails, who are just "gender-y."[15] It is precisely this kind of person that a linear "spectrum" model of gender can't accommodate. One of my favorite examples of this is drag king Delicio Del Toro who, while performing as an aggressive *luchador*

[Mexican wrestler] with mustache, hairy armpits, and bulging crotch, also reveals large breasts with silver pasties [nipple covers] midway into his performance. The use of pasties insists that the breasts are women's breasts—men are not expected to cover their nipples. Delicio does not sacrifice masculinity by adding exaggerated femininity; instead he uses the reveal to become *more* magnificent. He goes on to win the audience over even more by ejaculating the burrito that was hiding in his pants all over his adoring fans![16]

When I try to imagine what it means to be so gender-y, I immediately think of bearded drag queens. They may be highly feminine in physique, jewelry, and dress, but the beard is such a dominant marker of maleness that it interrupts seeing "a woman"; not that I necessarily see "a man" either. So gender-y! Through performance, drag artists can invent gender, mixing references and symbols to make possible alternative configurations of gender. This is politically risky work. Having a legible gender has become a prerequisite for being human,[17] and disrupting gender norms can render people dangerous, strange, or monstrous to mainstream eyes. Popular entertainment, from circuses and freak shows to award-winning films and TV shows, have historically paraded gender-nonconforming people—including bearded women!—as specimens, pathological killers, victims, and clowns.[18]

Instances when femininity and facial/body hair are deemed incompatible on the same body have rendered many people the target of public ridicule. In 2012, an unauthorized photograph of a Sikh woman named Balpreet Kaur was posted online and went viral, ridiculing her facial hair; in observance with her religion she does not trim her hair, including that on her face.[19] The same kind of online ridicule has pursued Alok Vaid-Menon, a poet, fashionista, and nonbinary activist who carefully details in their publications, interviews, and social media posts how their performed gender nonconformity has rendered them vulnerable to incessant attacks, many targeting their hairy body as incompatible with the fabulous feminine fashions they flaunt. KaMani Sutra, a South Indian drag queen who performs in ornate gilded garments, long silky black hair, and a full beard, has also documented the repeated attacks on her gender presentation. Three South Asian feminine figures, each wearing body and facial hair in very different contexts—in everyday life, for religious reasons, high fashion, and drag—fail to conform to the gender binary and therefore receive vitriolic antagonism.

It's worth remembering that there is an entire industry built around hair removal that seduces cis and trans people into seeing hairless adult bodies as more desirable. Also, femininity has been so systematically compounded with hairlessness that when we see feminine people moving through the world without facial hair, we're probably not seeing the artful, painful, and expensive *work* that has gone into rendering them beardless—shaving, waxing, makeup, plucking, electrolysis, bleaching, etc. Often this is an aspirational move toward approximating white ideals of femininity.[20] Being too hairy *or* too smooth *both* count as racialized measurements of gender, measurements perpetually calibrated against white bodies. Bearded drag queens are sometimes derided as "lazy," as not bothering to shave before performing, to do the painstaking work of producing femininity. However, what this dismissal fails to acknowledge is the creativity and innovation and risk it takes to imagine and paint a highly feminized, bearded face when society doesn't uplift this kind of gender, when magazines and films and tutorials don't visualize this version of beauty.

In a photograph titled *Hairy Breast* by genderqueer Tunisian digital drag artist Khookha McQueer, "a corseted [hairy] chest fills the frame, and two hands appear at the edges with fingers spread wide across the pectoral muscles." Khookha made *Hairy Breast* not only to critique binary beauty standards, but also Article 266 of the Tunisian penal code that criminalizes bawdy acts and public violations of decency.[21] A variety of laws and policies instituted under colonial rule, from those criminalizing crossdressing[22] to those enforcing decency, work to delimit gender. Drag, in its potential disruption of state sanctioned gender norms, can affirm our wonderfully strange bodies, invent new possibilities, and critique cultural and institutional regulations of the body.

How we see and do gender beyond such a binary framework *is* decolonial work. Dismantling such rigid epistemes that limit our perception to either/or categories can be understood as a form of decolonization because colonialism has been responsible for eradicating alternate gender/sex matrices and the knowledge systems they are a part of. Deviating from ideal forms of masculinity and femininity, or from familiar sex/gender systems, have justified settlement, extraction, and occupation. European colonial projects have identified the Other's failure to inhabit the sex/gender binary "properly" as a rationale for "civilizing" unruly others—East Asians were characterized as hyper-feminine, Bengalis as effeminate, Sikhs as militant, Middle Easterners as simultaneously sexually repressed *and* ravenous, Africans as hypermasculine, Southeast Asians as wild, and Native Americans as dangerous sodomites.[23]

These value judgements have been cultural *and* scientific, i.e., based on gender *and* sex. British colonials arriving in India in the early nineteenth century deemed the draped, unstitched clothes that Indian men wore too feminine, too colorful, and too similar to what women wore. The stitched garments that the British wore—pants and skirts—differentiated gender more rigidly.[24] This cultural difference was interpreted by colonizers as a lack of civilization; the perceived male effeminacy was taken to be a sign of weakness, and became a justification for imposing European moralities on the subcontinent.

Sex differentiation too was grounds for racial governance. You might be familiar with phrenology, the bogus science of brain and skull sizes that was used to justify settler colonialism by demonstrating empirical differences between Black and white people.[25] This was one aspect of racial science, a nineteenth-century field of study that measured more than just skulls to prove biological, and thus moral, difference between racial groups. Using "comparative anatomy," colonial scientists measured Black women's buttocks and labia to compare them with white women's in order to confirm biological (and therefore cultural and moral) inferiority. This pseudoscience with completely specious methods determined that Black women had larger labia and therefore were not properly evolved to be sexually differentiated from men.[26] These are just two examples of many ways that colonialism uses a binary sex/gender system to monitor variation and manufacture truths about racial differences, thus authorizing white supremacy. These examples also help us understand that when drag artists play with costume or body proportions, they are in fact referencing and drawing on histories of colonial power, whether intentionally or not.

Gender and sexual differences mark racial others as improperly human, immoral, and therefore deserving of capture, conversion, reform, and occupation. The ongoing project of US empire, war and occupation in South and Southwest Asia, has produced research—commissioned by the US government—that presents gender and sexual formations there as perverse: repressed homosexuality, intergenerational homosexual desire, honor killings of women.[27] This unsophisticated and ahistorical gender and sexual analysis, mapped on to race and region, justifies bombings, military presence, and the extraction of natural resources and labor. Take for example the grotesque photos from the Abu Ghraib

prison in Iraq released in 2004. US soldiers took photos
of Iraqi prisoners in sexualized, particularly homoerotic,
positions; the white soldiers posed smiling and making
gestures of success and accomplishment. The composi-
tion of these photos tried to degrade and subjugate the
prisoners by suggesting they were sexually deviant. The
images also asserted the power of the US soldiers, in
upright and triumphant positions, expressing their dom-
ination over these sexual-racial Others.[28]

Conquest, as these photos evidence, compels the
colonizer to put on display their imagined version of the
sexual and gender perversity of the racialized Other. US
empire-building in the Americas systematically categorized and wiped out Native people's gender and sexual
practices that settlers deemed "perverse."[29] Black Studies
scholars argue that histories of enslavement have not
just gendered Black people, but have ungendered them,
made Black bodies mutable or "fungible," something
that can be many things, that can be flexible in service
to capitalist extraction.[30] Given this historical context,
they argue that performance, and particularly dress, have
been integral to making the racialized body legible or
palatable; dress and crossdressing have been urgent ways
of doing gender as a means of survival.[31] Across race and
region, scholars have given careful thought to the way

dress—from turbans to qipaos—has been a significant
means to reconstitute the raced-gendered-sexed body.[32]

The legacy of British colonial law in India continues
to render transgender postcolonial subjects vulnerable.
In 1871, British lawmakers introduced the "Criminal
Tribes Act" that categorized certain people based on
religion, region, and caste as "habitually criminal," giving authorities a wide berth to arrest them, especially
if they were found outside the limited geography they
were confined to.[33] Included in this category were *hijras*,
transfeminine people often named a "third gender."
While the Act no longer persists, the stigma it cultivated around hijras does. Further, recent policies such as
the Karnataka Police Act 36A, introduced in 2011, have
been modeled on the Criminal Tribes Act.[34] 36A gave
police permission to arrest hijras when they exit their
residential neighborhoods—hijras often rely on begging
and sex work for income, and therefore require urban
mobility and access to public space for their survival.

I put "third gender" above in quotations because
this idiom, referring to hijras, muxes, *mahu*s, katho-
eys, etc., only becomes "third" in relation to the
Euro-Western binary. Other matrices of gender certainly exist. We might look to contemporary US
Black and Latinx Ballroom culture that has a six-part

(and ever-changing) gender system—butch queens up in drag, femme queens, butches, women, men/trade, butch queens.[35] These categories emerge through complex arrangements of biological sex, performed gender, and sexual roles.[36] We see other "genderscapes" or *phet* in Thailand that feature kathoey, *tom*, gay, female, and male.[37] To be clear, I'm not arguing that these arrangements are better than western binary formations, or that they don't traffic in familiar notions of masculinity or femininity for the purpose of distributing power and controlling equity. I offer them simply to demonstrate that other sex/gender configurations exist in the face of a binary structure that is widely taken for granted. European colonialism's interest in securing binary gender as the global norm was, and continues to be, a means of differentiating white bodies from colonial others, and it has eradicated some of these other matrices, physically (targeting gender-nonconforming children in settler schools for Native children in North America)[38] and in our everyday knowledge formations (for example, census data collection that only allows M and F options).

If the gender binary is made so sacred through the colonial violences of science, representation, and policing, undoing the binary can be a tactic of decolonization. It is, of course, not the only method of decolonizing gender; as I argue in the next chapter, subscribing to the binary or even mastering it by "performing realness" has its own merits for Black, Brown and trans people— safety, income, and joy. I want to emphasize the joy part here. For some of us, materially manifesting gender, binary or not, does bring delightful sensations when psychic fantasy comes to life. When I see LaWhore in the mirror, and not Kareem, I do take pleasure; she blushes, she pouts, she poses, she takes selfies. It's a pleasure only magnified when bouncers open the club door for her and bartenders rush to hand her a cocktail. It's a pleasure akin to what I feel after a visit to the barber, when my hair and beard are perfectly faded, when I feel like I'm somewhat succeeding at masculinity. I pout, I pose, I take selfies. As coercive as gender binaries can be, there is too an abundance of joy in approximating and achieving realness. To quote Gia Gunn, "Let me feel my oats!"

Binaries exist in many cultural contexts, but the punitive power of the gender binary as enforced by western colonial knowledge-making projects has secured itself as a kind of global norm. Drag has many potentials to bust binaries in order to restore and invent abundant possibilities of embodiment and selfhood decimated by colonialism. One example is the work of Cree artist Kent Monkman, who uses drag to revisit colonial misconceptions of Native American genders. In 1837, American lawyer George Catlin created "Dance to the Berdash," a painting that ridicules the reverence Indigenous people have for *berdache*, the figure he describes as "a man dressed in woman's clothes . . . he [the berdache] is driven to the most servile and degrading duties, which he is not allowed to escape."[39] Catlin, working only in a binary, could not fathom berdaches as being of their own gender, and was particularly disdainful of Native people's reverence for this figure.

Monkman, a Cree two-spirit visual and performance artist, crafts a response to Catlin's painting with his own dance to the berdache. Styled as his drag persona Miss Chief Eagle Testickle, he performs a tribute to these feminine figures in a 2010 music video called "Dance to Miss Chief," a follow up to a 2008 gallery installation titled "Dance to the Berdache."[40] The music video shows Miss Chief: slim, muscular, flat-chested, draped in beads and red fabric, long sexy legs exposed, with loose hair blowing in the wind against a black empty background, dancing with fluid movements to techno music. The footage cuts between her and stereotypical depictions of Native people in commercial film, dispelling the archaic memory of Indigenous people in popular imagination with this techno-dancing, fabulously styled berdache. Directly riffing on Catlin's condescending imagery, Miss Chief shows us that drag can restore complexity to Indigenous gender matrices; she unapologetically dances *to* the berdache, and then to Miss Chief (herself), positioning herself as the berdache and establishing continuity between historical genders and her own. Far from attempting to recover an authentic Indigenous figure, Miss Chief combines Native ritual and queer club cultures to invent gender and perform critique simultaneously.

While Catlin dismissed Indigenous gender forms as ridiculous and embarrassing, Monkman uses the aesthetics of queer nightlife, fabulous and femme, to disrupt the fixed formula used to interpret Indigenous genders. But, like Catlin, performers in the drag scene are also complicit in constricting gender categories, relegating some drag artists as second-tier or derivative of "real drag." Below, I explore how gender categories are entrenched, resisted, and reinvented in drag communities.

Drag's Gender Systems

While we think of LGBTQ spaces as inclusive and welcoming, gender binaries have firmly entrenched themselves in drag communities, and a whole taxonomy of *types* of drag artists has developed that relies on but also struggles with binary terms. Between 1995 and 2018, The Stud, a legendary San Francisco drag bar with a punk ethos, hosted the Miss Faux Queen Pageant. Terms like "faux queen" and "bio queen" emerged to refer to cisgender women who perform in drag, exaggerating feminine features like hips, breasts, facial contour, and hair much like drag queens do. If a woman has large breasts that produce a feminine silhouette, she still might use the technologies drag queens do to accentuate them for performance: wrapping duck tape around her torso to press them together so that they stand higher, and contouring the chest to make her cleavage look deeper. However, this differentiation between "faux queens" and "drag queens," one based on sex, authenticates feminine drag by cisgender men as the *real* drag.

These terminologies affect how drag shapes community. When I was twenty-six years old, living in Chicago, I co-founded *Jai Ho!* at my favorite bar, Big Chicks. I was looking for a South Asian drag queen to headline the first party and spoke to an elder queer Pakistani activist named Ifti Nasim. I had heard about parties in Ifti's living room filled with drag and dance. But when I asked him whether any of his drag queen friends would perform, he laughed at me, "These girls don't want to be mistaken for men!" He was referring to a broad spectrum of feminine people who wanted to be seen and desired as women. The working assumption that the authentic gender beneath the drag queen's stage persona is a "really a man" creates cleavages in the queer community; it means people must perform in different pageants, or under different categories.[41] Alternative pageants have indeed emerged for fat queens, queens of color, and older queens, because of the advantage white gay thin young cisgender men hold. Some transgender women who perform in the drag scene refer to themselves as "showgirls." By avoiding the term "drag," these trans women deflect the assumption that they are "cross-dressing," that what is under their stage persona is "really a man."

At The Stud's 2003 annual drag queen competition, not the one just for faux queens, faux queen Fauxnique won out over gay men and transgender women, offering us a reminder that the "faux" moniker is not less than or derivative of other kinds of drag. Faux queens, showgirls, and drag queens traffic in similar aesthetics. They shop for gowns and jewelry and breastplates and makeup and wigs at the same places. Femininity is not something only or already attached to female bodies, nor is masculinity only made by men; they are rather shared resources people of many genders work with.[42]

But why engage in gender play at all? Generally, I think people are by nature fascinated by the mutability of the body, of its capacity to be many things, even many genders. However, for gender and sexual minorities, the stakes of performing gender feel quite different. Knowing that our desires and sense of self deviate from the dominant mold, we become attuned to the ways we should or shouldn't act. We inadvertently develop a study of gender and the body as a mode of survival. In this way, gender becomes a form of knowledge, a currency for LGBTQ people even before they've read a book like this one that argues that gender is indeed a form of currency. Drag, a performance form that centers the manipulation of gender on stage, becomes an attractive genre to gender and sexual minorities to both witness and participate in because we already "get it." Many of us have been disciplined all our lives for not conforming to expected gender roles. Others have felt stifled or inauthentic in the way we subscribed to gendered expectations. Drag can be a means of reconciling or interfacing with our former selves, collecting and trying on the pieces of gender we left behind to avoid being made fun of, to deflect violence and shame, to be desirable, to please our parents, teachers, and friends.[43] Touching the past through drag allows for new, messy, and exciting ways of rethinking our bodies in the present.

Drag is also an opportunity to interrupt gender altogether, what is sometimes called "genderfuck" or "tranimal" drag. Reflecting on the variety of drag she has witnessed, drag that she's found titillating, fun, and sexy, Sarah Hankins writes,

> How can a mode of gender performance decline to perform gender? I have tipped Katya Zamolodchikova as a cat (a large, sexy cat), Johnny Blazes as a zombie removing hir/its own body parts as ze lurches down the catwalk at Jacques' Cabaret, and TraniWreck cast principal Madge of Honor performing as a . . . thing wrapped in terrifying black plastic, standing still under a spotlight.[44]

I too have watched drag shows with lip-synching minotaurs, skyscrapers, icebergs, Loch Ness monsters, alien Diva Plavalaguna, lobsters, and many cats—if the 2019 movie version of *Cats* has one merit, it taught us that cats can be peculiarly sexy. It strikes me that even when watching animals or objects dancing, I can still think of the performers as sexy. This tells me that there is room in my imagination to interpret and desire bodies beyond gender.[45]

Drag can be a place to *make* gender, to make new genders possible, to reinvent the body.[46] The repeated embodiment of and exposure to animals, objects, and signifiers of fantasy (aliens, mythological creatures, etc.) can un-train our singular lens of interpretation and allow us to imagine gender differently not just on stage but everywhere we look and live.

For trans people, drag is sometimes the first place that they come into awareness about their gender dissidence, or where they are allowed to inhabit what has only been fantasy. As a playground, a site of leisure and fun, drag lowers the bar for trying on genders that do not seem permissible in other facets of life. It also allows us to find new comfort with ways of presenting that can sediment into identity. In Indonesia, *waria* are feminine-spirited people who were assigned male at birth. They engage in practices of beautification and glamorous aesthetics called *déndong*. While self-identified warias differentiate themselves from gay men, they also suggest that when gay men engage in the feminine decadence of déndong—doing drag for example—these men's spirit might change, that they might become waria too.[47]

For trans women who want or need to pass as female every day by conforming to normative gender expectations, drag is an opportunity to try on other kinds of femininity that they don't regularly have access to in their quotidian survival work. One example is Diana

Devor, the drag persona of a thirty-eight-year-old, Mexican American transsexual woman in central Texas who is livelier, sassier, and more vocally activist on stage than her everyday professional self: "The character [provides] a less conditional matrix than the one of her daily living in which her gender and race were sources of discrimination."[48] Devor says about her performances, "I try to teach to people in shows, whether I'm helping or I'm talking about it, is that I'm not ashamed of my size, I'm not ashamed of my race, I'm not ashamed of my age."[49]

Diana Devor makes clear that drag is a place for embodied imagination in a world that wants to crush minority subjects, our bodies and our psyches, through racism, ageism, fatphobia, sexism, and transphobia. While there are categories and frameworks in the LGBTQ drag world that subscribe to a Euro-western gender binary, "kings and queens" for example, the actual scene of performance offers opportunity for radical self-invention in the face of systems that want to wipe out beautiful forms of variation. Also, her claims are an important reminder that what is at stake when putting the body on stage is *not just gender.* Her gender, beauty, and value are measured through race, body size, and age; it is through all these axes collectively that she becomes legible as a woman, as a drag queen, as desirable, or friendly, or fun, or important to listen to. This leads us into our next chapter, to understand that gender is never an isolated category of identity, but always made in tandem with others.

Chapter 2

BEYOND GENDER: RACE, REALNESS, AND WHAT COUNTS AS DRAG

In Texas, it is not uncommon to see a drag tribute to Selena Quintanilla, the young Tejana music legend who was suddenly killed in 1995. The first Selena impersonation I saw was by Kelly Kline, Austin's very own "bisexual, bilingual, bipolar" Latina trans drag queen. According to Kelly, though Selena died at age twenty-three, she remains an icon of Mexican American working-class mobility, achieving national pop stardom as a Brown woman with unapologetically ethnic fashion singing in Spanish.[50] In a now-notorious performance at a San Antonio bar, a (non-Latina) white drag queen began her performance by exiting a coffin on stage, Selena rising from the dead, much to the displeasure of the mostly Latinx audience.[51]

The white camp aesthetic, to laugh at powerful icons and symbols, failed here not because the audience had no sense of humor, but because Selena is a repository of sentiment and possibility for a historically marginalized people, particularly working-class Mexican Americans. The subordination of Tejanx people stems from the contestations between Spanish and US empire-building projects over Texas, and it is further entrenched by the ever-expanding securitization of the US–Mexico border and the precarious labor conditions that emerged under NAFTA. Selena's rise to stardom beckoned to people who were perpetually denied social and national citizenship; she reflected a body, sound, and movement that felt familiar. Performing as zombie Selena misses the point as to *why* she is so popular.

The Selena tributes I have watched have been just that: tributes studied from recordings of her live performances and music videos, paying attention to every detail, mimicking her cumbia choreography, spangled purple jumpsuit, and even the most specific hand gestures she made to emphasize the instrumentation. One performer I saw in Austin even had a Band-Aid around her pointer finger, exactly as Selena did at her final performance at the Houston Astrodome. The audience went giddy in excitement when they noticed that detail! Just as satirizing gender has the potential to address the violence that gender norms inflict on our psyche and body, so too mimicking it *with accuracy* has the capacity to access the gifts that artists of color, particularly women and gender non-conforming artists, have gifted minoritarian people. Their own survival and innovation in industries that never promised them success remains a repository of possibility.

What I'm trying to show above is that the stakes of performing gender are predicated also on race, class, migration, and colonialism. When performers of color get on stage, they come to stand in for more than just their own artistic body, they bear the burden of representing people like them.[52] Also, when performers draw on the persona or music or sartorial style of Black and Brown celebrities, those stars' racialized histories too come to matter. Additionally, the audience, their individual and collective social positions, dictate with what sense of longing or affiliation they watch.

The consequence of putting one's solo body on stage is quite different for people of color, who are always interpreted through those colonial histories of gender that haunt them. Colonial histories have marked people of color variously as exotic, primitive, oversexed, effeminate, asexual, hypermasculine, etc., and these assumptions are at play, whether we register it consciously or not, when we perform *and* when we watch a show. Drag is not *just* the manipulation or transformation of gender, but of so many other categories of embodiment as well. This chapter places the onus on drag to not only grapple with gender hierarchies but other axes of history and embodiment that co-constitute gender. When I say "co-constitute" I mean that gender can't be isolated as a separate category of identity, different from race, ethnicity, religion, class, etc. Rather, the way our gender works in the world, the way people see us, the way we experience oppression or acquire access, is predicated on these other social positions. To understand race and gender on stage as co-constitutive expands the category of drag beyond what has been foreclosed by forms of whiteness. Drag isn't just about gender, but so many other facets of our being, our social and political histories!

Race, and racist assumptions, are already gendering performers *before* they "get into drag." For example, Asian men's bodies are read as feminine even when not "in drag." Colonial presence in Asia has long been justified through notions of paternalism, positioning white men as fathers, husbands, and saviors. This has rendered Asian men "feminine," "young," or "wild."[53] Whether it is the light hairless skin or smaller frame of *some* Asian men's bodies, or the "graceful" drape of South Asian men's clothing,[54] Asian men were and are regularly associated with femininity, or with not being fully evolved into civilized masculinity.

The persistence of this colonial mentality shows up in drag pageantry. In his study of gay Asian American men and drag queens on the US West Coast, sociologist C. Winter Han found that white queer people see Asian

American performers as having an unfair advantage in drag pageants simply because they are "already feminine."[55] Masculinity is fetishized by many gay men; to be Asian in predominantly white gay men's spaces, to be "already feminine," means to lack sexual capital. Asian American men, when not in drag, get very little attention in the larger gay scene, except as fetish objects, because they are deemed *too* feminine, whether they personally identify that way or not. As such, Asian American drag queens in Han's study—many of whom were subject to everyday sexual racism—would celebrate their wins in pageants, a rare moment when the legacy of Asian feminization works in their favor and allows them to feel valuable and important in the gay community.[56]

Colonial rhetorics similarly fabricated the supposition that Black bodies are already masculine, and that Black male and female bodies were not properly evolved to be distinguishable from each other. This association of Blackness with hypermasculinity inadvertently works in drag king scenes to make Black performers more "successful" in their portrayal of masculinity.

In the nineties, New York City enjoyed a lively drag king scene in the circuit of lesbian bars that included HerShe Bar and Club Casanova.[57] At king competitions held at these bars, butch Black women could win a competition presenting in their everyday masculine attire. White drag kings, on the other hand, put a lot of effort into their visual transformation by developing characters, concepts, and costumes.[58] Butch Black women strutting around in their everyday wear were winning over drag kings who had crafted elaborately conceived numbers, and this left some performers conflicted: what counts as true drag? Like the Asian American drag queens who had an "unfair advantage," here too, blackness amplified masculinity, was already masculine, and left white performers perplexed at their losses.

I want to reiterate that in their everyday lives, queer and trans people of color in the US rarely benefit from being hyperfeminized, hypermasculinized, or hypersexualized. In fact these genderings put them in the way of systemic, social, and sexual violence. Drag becomes a moment to turn these violent projects on their heads, to wield these imperial histories for small, but not inconsequential gain. The opportunity to feel good, famous, important, or sexy on stage with our trans and queer peers is affirming and life-giving. Sometimes there's even a cash prize!

Keeping it Real

Scholars of drag often observe that artists of color are more likely to invest in the aesthetics of realness, as Latinx performers do with Selena. While drag is famously invested in playing with and dismantling gender binaries, there are some contexts in which it seems particularly valuable for people of color to commit to a "real" aesthetic rather than make fun of or deconstruct gender binaries.

Early in his career, Black disco legend Sylvester was part of a radical California-based drag collective known as The Cockettes. In their 1971 film "Tricia's Wedding," the ensemble parodies the wedding of Tricia Nixon and Edward Cox at the White House, lampooning the snobbery of political elites, peppering their performance with boob jokes and genital reveals. However, Sylvester's performances as sex symbol and songstress Eartha Kitt and as Coretta Scott King, wife of the late Martin Luther King, are much more graceful and somber than the rest of the outrageous cast.[59] This tactic, to not reach toward camp or genderfuck in the ways that other Cockettes did, suggests that Sylvester understood the constraints these Black women already lived with by entering the public eye, that their femininity was already up for contestation, that they didn't need further "exposure" through ribald parody.[60]

One of the reasons we might consider the stakes of realness in performing Black and Latinx celebrities is because of the burden of representation they often carry. To make fun of white celebrities is to make fun of their specific quirks and foibles—they enjoy the privilege of individuality. However, to lampoon Kitt or King, iconic as they are, runs the risk of laughing at Black people more broadly.

In addition to the serious aesthetics of celebrity impersonation by people of color, "real" aesthetics of racialized drag appear in the Ballroom scene. Balls are competitive social events in which collectives known as "houses" vie for trophies in a variety of runway and dance-based performance categories. In the Black and Latinx Ball scene, "realness" describes the ability to walk the runway and face a panel of judges in a sartorial category with precision. So while the participants may be queer, when they serve realness in a "schoolboy" or "Wall Street" category, "realness is achieved if the competitor *unmarks* himself as sexually queer through his gender performance."[61] Realness reveals the constructed natures of race, class, and gender by being able to replicate them meticulously, assembling these identities on the body through dress, gait, pose, and gesture such that they replicate what moves through the world as seemingly authentic or natural.

Realness is also part of a survival toolkit. In the "femme queen realness" category, trans women exhibit their bodies to be scrutinized by judges at the Ball for how perfectly they pass as female, for the precision with which they've erased visual traces of maleness.[62] Outside the Ball, to pass is to be able to avoid transphobic harassment and violence in public. In queer worlds that celebrate subversion and mess, realness may seem old-fashioned in its adherence to binary gender norms. However, realness is an urgent means for some trans people to bring their bodies into the world in ways that align with their sense of self. It also invites others, strangers and loved ones alike, to see their gender on their terms; if we remember that gender is made through performance, then accomplishing realness can invite others to experience us the way we know ourselves. Further, knowing the outsized violence that trans women of color are subjected to, the Ball scene teaches us that realness is both playful performance *and* a place where survival strategies are taught and rehearsed.[63] Even digital platforms, which we valorize as a site for experimenting with identity and anonymity, in their surveillant mission to gather data on and closely track users, require trans people to perform realness.[64]

Even though patrons attend drag shows to enjoy the illusions of gender, audiences sometimes insist on assuring themselves that the gender transgressions they're witnessing are only for play, are not real. Don't be surprised when you see audiences at drag shows touch performers' breasts, butts, and crotches without asking, usually padded with some kind of fabricated material: foam, socks, silicon bra inserts, rubber dildos. This common act of touching assures the spectator that the artist's gender performance is indeed "fake."[65] It also relies on the myth that any kind of trans body is is oversexed and available for touch without consent, that their gender performance is in service of sexual pleasure. You'll often hear drag show hosts explain consent at their shows, especially when they determine that there are a significant number of straight folks in the audience—not knowing the shared codes of the space can produce complicated contestations over identity and meaning.

This was certainly the case at a 1998 *laelae* drag show that Kalissa Alexeyeff, a scholar of gender and sexuality in the Pacific, attended. Laelae is a gender category in some Pacific islands that captures a variety of alternatives to the masculine-feminine binary. At this laelae drag show, performers drew on both local traditions of cross-dressing, as well as global drag pageantry styles to make jokes and to look sexy. Their self-descriptions, props, and costumes referenced domestic life and motherhood, playing with local ideas of femininity, rather than grand visions of fame and glamor; the way they moved on the catwalk was "sensual without being overtly sexual."[66] As the night's performances moved between registers of the local and the global, the audience had to move with it, to track the humor and fashion through these shifting understandings of what gender references were being enacted.

However, one tourist's lack of familiarity with both Indigenous feminine performance and queer modes of conduct spoiled the mood. One of the night's performers, Lady Posh, directed her flirtations at two men from the audience. The man who had grown up there in Rarotonga was exuberant and buffoon-like, responding to Lady Posh's advances with glee and playful admiration. The tourist, a visitor from Melbourne, was not familiar with the kind of play-flirtation that his counterpart and other local men in the audience were. He took her seduction seriously, and his "overtly masculine sexual movements [made the queen] uncomfortable, and the audience's reaction suggested that it detracted from the entertainment."[67]

It is important to remember that gender is produced *in dialogue* with others, between audience and performer, and that people arrive at the drag show with different notions of how to decipher and translate gender. Following the cues of others, especially those who are regulars at a drag show, can help decipher the norms around flirting, tipping, and touch.

What I've tried to get at so far is that there is *so much more* going on in drag performance than simply gender or gender crossing, and a performance's meanings are constituted between performer, audience, location, and the historical specters of colonialism that shape how we interpret each other. Even in the performance of "realness," what we might think of as the most conforming enactment of binary gender, race and class become valuable points through which to evaluate artistry and to consider the stakes of putting gender on the body. I'm so insistent on this matter because if gender crossing is the only measure of "success" in drag, we create conditions under which people who do gender and gender crossing differently might not be seen as doing drag. Let me explain . . .

What counts as drag?

When my student told me about the stranger's reaction to LaWhore's performance, that "they're not real drag queens," it reminded me of another instance I'd read about. Queer Studies scholar Jasbir Puar, attending the Diva festival in Trinidad that features drag acts, found that while people cheered excitedly for Black and white performers, the couple performing Indian dance numbers received less applause. When she asked audience members why they thought the reception for this dancing couple was less enthusiastic, Puar was told, "they were simply performing an 'ethnic' dance."[68] While other artists lip-synched to Tina Turner, Toni Braxton, and Patti LaBelle, this Indian couple's choice of songs from Indian and Indo-Trinidadian films strayed too far from what was seen as legibly drag.

I want to think about how things become "not drag," to help those of us on the other side of the performance—audiences, critics, scholars, witnesses, judges, curators—loosen our frameworks of drag to include more forms of performance and people. Doing so relinquishes the hold cis white able-bodiedness has over our understanding of gender and over drag. Disability critics argue that forms of gender performance—certain kinds of movement, makeup, scents—are inaccessible to some fat and disabled people.[69] The kind of athleticism and flexibility that is so highly praised in drag performance—jumps, splits, cartwheels, and dips, often in high heels—is unavailable to people with mobility impairments, and the intensity of sound and bodies in nightclub spaces can be an unbearable sensorial experience.

Drag can also be quite unaffordable; it's not uncommon to hear US drag artists remind their audiences how expensive their art is—"It takes a lot of money to look this cheap!" In the wake of *RuPaul's Drag Race*, drag has become even *more* expensive as performers are encouraged to show off "polished" looks purchased from artisans that make costumes, jewelry, and wigs, rather than wear outfits "off the rack." Drag is expensive but vastly under-compensated, which is why many drag artists have other full-time sources of income. Limited resources also limit gender performance. In South Africa, drag by white queens performing in upscale urban nightclubs is much more gender-conforming than that by Black and Colored queens from the townships: "that peculiar androgyny of township drag [is] borne of scant resources and much imagination, nodding at gender inversion with no more than a frilly shirt, a pair of garish earrings, a touch of rouge, a pair of low-heeled pumps, a third-hand wig."[70]

In other cases, this genderfuck drag emerges not out of the lack of resources, but because it draws its referents from other gender systems:

When [South African drag queen] Belinda Qaqamba
Ka-Fassie dresses in drag, she doesn't typically go for
the sequins and feather boas worn by performers on
RuPaul's Drag Race [. . .] Ka-Fassie might put on a
dress that resembles the white blanket typically worn
by boys at a traditional male circumcision ritual,
called ulwaluko, and she might add a multicolored
headpiece and beaded stick, both handmade and used
by brides. It's a very deliberate choice made by black
drag queens from townships who are celebrating
their roots and challenging dress codes for men and
women through their traditional apparel.

Whether born of the limiting resource of money or the
abundant resources of Xhosa dress, the innovative gender configurations of makeshift drag by people of color
is often co-opted by white influencers and sold back to
the world as "fashion."[71]

We see this kind of androgyny on Vine, Instagram,
and TikTok videos of young low-income kids in
Southeast Asia and Brazil filming in rural spaces.
They read as prepubescent boys, but by tying bricks to
their feet to create heels, refashioning palm leaves into
gowns, and lip-synching with such accuracy that their
faces conjure the songstress, they invent and remake
their gender and age. Perhaps most famous of these
digital drag junior divas is Thailand's Madaew, whose
sartorial innovations styled from baskets, buckets, and

wires has earned the fashionista over 70,000 followers on Instagram. The ability to be "fabulous,"[72] to gesture beyond glamor with minimal resources, reminds us that drag need not rely on the expensive accoutrements of gender.

Further, while the trimmings of femininity are commercially available—jewelry, glittery makeup, cutlets, corsets, wigs—accessories to masculinize the body are not commonly sold. Indu Antony is a Bangalore-based photographer, who makes work about the politics and aesthetics of gender. She worked on two consecutive shoots, one titled *Bitch Please!* featuring amateur drag queens, and another called *ManiFest*, a series of Indian drag kings posing as famous pop-culture figures. The stylist for Antony's two series notes that while it was easy for him to assemble outfits for the drag queens, he had to be inventive about what to use to comfortably and affordably bind breasts, stuff crotches, and create facial hair because none of these items were easily available in retail marketplaces.[73]

Fabricating gender can be expensive, but gender can also be made simply through the body, through pose, gesture, and dance. *Kothi*s in India are male-assigned, feminine-identifying people, often from working-class backgrounds. Day to day, many present in men's clothing and may have facial hair. However, kothis can be exceptionally feminine when they dance; in their menswear they are still able to transform gender through movement, through bends of the wrist, flicks of the hip, delicate articulations of the fingers, pursing of the lips. In India we're seeing a fast-burgeoning drag scene, populated by middle-class, dominant-caste, and elite men, women, and non-binary people who can afford heavy makeup, sequined outfits, false eyelashes, and photoshoots, who run slick Instagram accounts. These seemingly "new" outspoken drag artists become the "ambassadors of queerness" for the community.[74] But kothis, hijras, and other transfeminine people, many of whom occupy subordinate caste positions, have been dancing in public at Pride marches and festivals, have been spokespersons for the movement, and have been entertaining the community well before the new fabulous drag queen.[75]

What would it take to think about feminine kothi dance—often barefoot in pants and a men's shirt—*as* drag? Dance critic Naomi Bragin offers us the term "corporeal drag" to name the brilliant manipulation of gender through bodily movement for pleasure and visibility in queer and trans community, what we see in dance forms like waacking and voguing.[76] Waacking

emerges out of 1970s Los Angeles' Black queer club
scene. Dancers reanimated the glamorous gestures of
old-Hollywood into elaborate arm movements and
complex poses. Voguing is a dance form that emerges
from the 1980s Harlem Ballroom scene. It takes the styl-
ized postures of fashion modeling, a repertoire invested
in visualizing the white body as superior and elegant.[77]
By setting the angles and shapes into motion on Black
and Brown bodies, voguing and waacking reorganize
the dancer's gender,[78] they do drag through movement
rather than dress or makeup: "The voguing body . . .
is an otherworldly body unleashed, moving against
the rules of gender and physics before exploding into
collapse with wild grace onto her one leg."[79] In the
Auckland Ball scene, voguing is precisely the practice
that allows Pasifika queer people the room to confound
and reinvent dance traditions that are deeply stratified
by gender.[80]

I bring up kothi dance *as* drag not to force it into a
westernized category, but to recognize its brilliant artistry that belongs on the stages that celebrate drag. I also
place it in the world of drag because identities move and
shift. People can be kothi and gay,[81] trans and gay,[82] *bakla*
and trans,[83] travestí and trans.[84] Identities code-switch
as people move across borders; the same queen might

perform in trans pageants in the Philippines, but in drag pageants in Canada, someone may be kothi in peri-urban areas, but gay in the city. Movement, of the kinesthetic body and of bodies across borders, is crucial to shaping gender and identity, and to keep drag dynamic we must pay attention to how and where bodies move. Gender is often described through visual logics, and we don't always think about or have the language to name how important movement is to making meaning through the body.[85]

Speaking of dance, not all drag needs twirls, dips, poses, kicks, and catwalks, nor should it. I'll take a gorgeous, still and staid, excellent execution of a ballad over splits and dips *any day*. That said, not all bodies can easily slip into gender *through* movement; mobility impairments might restrict the intricate posturing so central to executing gender along binary logics. It's essential that we keep our logics of *what drag is* and *where it belongs* supple; doing so offers more opportunities to encounter drag and more frames through which to appreciate artistry. Nightlife spaces can be especially inaccessible: dark, smoky, and without ramps. DJs are at the heart of club spaces, often prioritizing music in ways that do not serve the pleasure of deaf clubgoers.[86] While drag shows in clubs and bars privilege singing, lip-synch, and dynamic dance styles, deaf Latinx drag queen duo Casavina and Selena Minogue use YouTube as the platform that better shows off their social commentary and kitschy skits.[87] Digital drag has seen a boom during the COVID-19 pandemic, but we cannot forget that deaf and disabled artists were putting this medium to its best use as a space for queer artistry and collectivity before nightclubs took a pause in early 2020. Additionally, for artists working in locations where access to live venues celebrating queer and trans artmaking are limited, the virtual sphere has been an important opportunity to extend and grow their practice and audience.[88]

It is possible that my suggestion that *more* things be permitted into the category of drag—cross-dressing traditions, various kinds of trans performance, scrappy transformations with limited resources, movement styles, web-based content—might be its own colonizing move. My goal in inviting other forms of performance into the category of drag is to advocate for the redistribution of resources that neoliberal, able-bodied, white-washed drag draws away from queer and trans performers and genres that don't work in this mode. As drag enjoys growing interest, my gesture to call more things drag is to push festival curators, show producers, and club owners to invite (and pay) more kinds of people on to their stages, perhaps even to rethink the location, format, or medium of exhibition. I also want audiences, critics, and scholars to pay attention not only to the visual/sartorial illusion but to the kinesthetic/choreographic nature of gender, as well as to the many other axes of identity that drag artists mobilize. By doing so, we credit, honor, and pay systemically marginalized cultural producers with the creativity and excellence that has often been stolen from them.

Colonial Collusions

Before I get all hopeful, I must also acknowledge that drag, in its project of impersonations, also has the habit of entrenching enduring inequalities. The charge often levied against drag performance, particularly drag queens, is that the genre on the one hand parodies femininity and thus mocks women, and on the other, it manifests versions of femininity that are unrealistic for everyday women to embody. While some drag acts are complicit in misogyny, these wholesale arguments rest on the assumption that femininity belongs only to female-assigned people. I've shown in Chapter 1 that there is value in rethinking the sex/gender binary system in order to understand that masculinity and femininity can be shared by different people, rather than be naturalized in particular sexed bodies. To dismiss drag as misogynist does not reckon with performers' actual experience of gender, their deep engagement with the ruptures, strangeness, and pleasure of putting gender onto the body. Pathbreaking work in lesbian studies theorizing butch-femme coupling argues that purposeful play within the codes of binary gender systems allows for pleasure and creativity rather than capitulation to heteronorms.[89] To be clear, I am saying that drag is not inherently misogynist—some drag artists and performances can be, but as a genre it is not inherently so. In fact many of the drag queens I discuss in this book are using their platform to critique violence inflicted on the basis of gender.

Just as *some* drag can replicate sexism, there are ways that drag can and does participate in entrenching racial hierarchy. Trans historian Susan Stryker's research on the Bohemian Grove argues that racialized cross-dressing can be understood as an embodied rehearsal of the imperial politics of US expansion into the Pacific.[90] The Bohemian Grove was an all-male elite social club established in the late nineteenth century in the San Francisco Bay Area, where politicians, diplomats, and future presidents could schmooze and network. Amongst the club members, but ranked lower as associate members, were artists who often provided entertainment that was central to the perks of membership. Some of these performances were commissioned to celebrate club members' new postings in the Pacific, and they often involved minstrel-style drag shows that mocked the feminized destinations to which the white diplomats and entrepreneurs were posted. In these all-male spaces, racialized drag was essential in feminizing foreign destinations in ways that conferred paternalistic powers on the white men about to travel there.

During the nineteenth-century Gold Rush in California, drag also played a part in securing white supremacy.[91] White Americans flocked West in search of wealth, while also displacing and devastating Native populations. The influx of white men during the Gold Rush created gender imbalances—they didn't want to intermingle with Indigenous and Mexican women—that prompted new practices of cross-dressing at social dances. Sometimes gender crossing was performed with a simple handkerchief around the arm to designate the man was playing the part of a woman for the night. On other occasions, men wore women's garments and assumed feminine airs. Cross-dressing, however creative and playful, secured white supremacy by displacing Indigenous and Mexican women as desirable dance (and romantic) partners, and through mockery of other races by dragging in blackface. Further, social cross-dressing contrasted with the feminization of Chinese migrant workers. Where white men could take off their feminine costumes, Chinese men were marked in print media as naturally feminine in order to conscript them into domestic labor. These stigmatizations, casting them as improperly gendered, were central to justifying racial discrimination and eventually instituting laws that barred Asian migration into the US.

Even as Asia is staged as a monolithic elsewhere in the Bohemian Grove and Asians are rendered perversely gendered in Gold Rush California, drag acts in Asia have also reproduced colonial structures endemic to their respective nations. In Thai kathoey shows, performers stage Indigenous femininities that do not conform to aspirational whiteness, East Asian-ness, or upper-class light-skinned Thai-ness for humor or even mockery:

> In comedic burlesque or ribald routines, kathoey use country music to support their depictions of rural Thai womanhood as the foil of cosmopolitan urban respectability: what not to be. Such drag characters typically display rustic mismatched clothing, bad makeup, unkempt hair, excessive body hair, flat noses with large blackened nostrils, splotchy or wrinkled skin, and accessories such as woven baskets or paper and plastic bags. In other routines kathoey

divas may perform Western (white or black) and Chinese ballads, lip-synching in elegant costumes surrounded by casts of professional dancers. Such kathoey performances depict foreign femininity as beautiful, modern, and culturally inspiring, in contrast to the grotesque, backward forms of embodiment attributed to native Thai women.[92]

In the cross-dressed Indian ritual performances of Kuchipudi, known as *stree vesham*, dominant caste men claim expertise over femininity in ways that secure their caste and gender privilege.[93] Also, while white drag queens in South Africa can draw from a broad repertoire of Black and white divas to sing and lip-synch, "Black and Coloured performers are largely restricted to impersonating women of color."[94] These trends in the South African drag scene work to unmark whiteness, while hyper-racializing Black and Coloured people.

I've spent time in this chapter outlining the ways that race, ethnicity, location, class, disability matter to thinking about what drag artists are doing when they perform. More than simply conjuring gender, drag artists are relying on, navigating, and activating histories of colonialism as they present their bodies. In cases such as Sylvester's performance of Eartha Kitt or Kelly Kline's performance of Selena, they perform in ways that protect not only these celebrities, but also Black and

Brown people more generally. However, in examples such as the kathoey shows and Bohemian Grove, drag has the potential to ridicule colonized people. Drag can be capacious, but it can also be complicit in entrenching racial hierarchies, and there is no archive richer or more expansive than that of *RuPaul's Drag Race* to think through the art form's contradictory projects.

Start your engines . . .

Chapter 3

NEOLIBRULISM:
RUPAUL'S DRAG EMPIRE

With a net worth valued at almost 60 million dollars, RuPaul Charles, host of the Emmy Award-winning show *RuPaul's Drag Race*, is the world's most powerful drag artist. Michael Shulman, writing for *The New York Times*, described the TV show as "expanding into a mini-drag empire" and Evan Ross Katz for *Paper* magazine said, "RuPaul built himself an empire. Long may he reign."[95]

I take the language of "empire" here seriously. Empire is not just a euphemism for the scale and reach of RuPaul's influence, but also a project of accumulating power by managing both capital and knowledge, money and minds. Popular narratives attribute the increased visibility of drag in the global public sphere to RuPaul. But when the narrative pivots around this singular figure, positioning her as a pioneer, it displaces many forms of gender performance that exist outside her style of drag or well before her. The drag she is gifting the world is one that must be bought, and it is expensive! Additionally, her combination of self-promotion and self-actualization are wrapped in neoliberal models of professionalism, individual responsibility, and free markets.[96]

Across her career, RuPaul mobilizes whiteness in the form of the "Glamazon" to find success. As a Black performer in a racist nightlife and media culture of the eighties, she leans on whiteness as a means of finding mobility. However, as her career skyrockets, she does little to unsettle or question white aesthetics. Rather, she becomes the arbiter of perfection, professionalism, conformity, and even the gender binary. RuPaul lauds the capacity for drag to unmask the absurdity of gender binaries, but through her show and in her personal style she inadvertently confirms binaries rather than undoes them. *RuPaul's Drag Race*—shaped by RuPaul's hand, the showrunners, and network stations—reproduces the violent tendencies of empire in its capitulation to xenophobia, islamophobia, and fatphobia.

The first section of this chapter maps RuPaul's career and the growth of "RuPaul's Drag industrial complex," a multi-million-dollar industry of networked business ventures that pivot around RuPaul's fame.[97] Later, I describe how RuPaul and her show create a set of conditions that defer the responsibility of collective care that is so central to drag life and economy. And finally, I discuss scenes and narratives from *RuPaul's Drag Race* that capture the grotesque ways that race, religion, and Indigeneity are configured on the show, pointing to the strategies some contestants use to turn these problematics on their head.

RuPaul's Drag Industrial Complex

Legend has it, RuPaul was destined for fame even before her birth.

RuPaul Andre Charles was born in California in 1960 to working-class Black parents Ernestine Fontinette and Irving Charles; during her pregnancy, a psychic told Ernestine, "It's a boy, and he's going to be famous."[98] In the wake of her parents' divorce RuPaul journeyed to Atlanta at age fifteen to live with her older sister. It was in Atlanta that she attended a performing arts high school, started go-go dancing for New Wave bands, and saw her first drag queen, the legendary Crystal Labeija.

In Atlanta's punk and drag scenes, RuPaul started experimenting with style and gender, mixing glittery makeup, jock straps, thigh-high boots, and football shoulder pads to produce androgynous and genderfuck looks.[99] As she traveled between New York and Atlanta, she began to develop various feminine personae for herself: Bianca Cupcake Dinkins, the illegitimate daughter of NYC mayor David Dinkins; a Black transsexual street-hooker Soul Train dancer; and Blaxploitation film inspired ass-kicker Starrbooty.[100] Through the eighties,

RuPaul was the lead singer for a punk band called Wee Wee Pole, a go-go dancer and club kid at New York parties, and even had her own cable-access television show. For some of this time, she was also homeless, storing her belongings in the locker room of renowned East Village nightclub the Pyramid.[101] As RuPaul saw her peers graduate from the New York club scene to mainstream TV and radio, she became conscious of the ways that, as a Black, queer, gender-nonconforming artist, her experimental drag would not grant her the fame she pursued, the kind of fame that was promised by her mother's psychic.

In the early nineties, RuPaul launched herself as "Supermodel of the World." Instead of punk and androgynous aesthetics, RuPaul opted for sequined gowns, and blond hair coiffed high. She remembers this pursuit of fame:

> I said, I'm gonna do this in drag. Not only am I going to do this in drag, I'm going to do it in glamazon drag. And I'm going to take some of the sexual subversiveness out of it and make myself like a Disney caricature, so that Betty and Joe Beer Can won't feel threatened by the sexual aspects of drag. They won't be threatened by the fact that I'm actually mocking identity. That was the scientific combination that I used to break through to the mainstream.[102]

RuPaul leaned on the expertise of her friends Randy Barbato, Fenton Bailey, Mathu Andersen, and Zaldy Goco, all of whom became long-term collaborators, to restyle her into a more palatable (but still spectacular) self.[103] She cemented this new persona with the hit track "Supermodel (You Better Work)."[104] Take a break, give the song a listen! Or better yet, watch the music video on YouTube—it's a bop!

While this glamazon style earned RuPaul appearances in music videos, a talk show, and even a contract with MAC Cosmetics, it didn't lift her to global stardom as the psychic predicted. It was the launch of *RuPaul's Drag Race*, a reality TV show developed by Barbato and Bailey, that catapulted RuPaul to fame. After many rejections from several TV networks, the show eventually aired on Logo TV network in 2009 as a reality competition featuring ten drag queens vying for the title of "America's next drag superstar." The queens were expected to show off their "Charisma, Uniqueness, Nerve, and Talent" by sewing garments, styling looks, and improvising comedic sketches. Each week, a winner was chosen, and the bottom two queens had to lip-synch against each other for RuPaul to decide who would stay in the competition. Not only did *RuPaul's Drag Race* appeal to the queer audience of Logo TV, the show cultivated broader familiarity by emulating other successful TV competitions of the 2000s, specifically *Project Runway* and *America's Next Top Model*, and more tangentially *Fear Factor* and *Survivor*. RuPaul, in flamboyant tailored suits, played the show's Tim Gunn, advising the contestants toward success. On the runway, RuPaul appeared in her feminine regalia, makeup flawlessly painted on by Mathu Andersen, elaborate gowns designed by Zaldy, presiding over the competition à la Tyra Banks, and making the final judgement on who wins, and who goes home.

Largely following the format of Season One, the show is, as of 2023, in its fifteenth season, with eight additional *All Star* seasons featuring past favorites from the show competing against each other. In 2017, the show migrated from Logo TV to VH1, doubling its viewership from the previous season to a million;[105] in 2023 the show moved to MTV. Franchises of the show appear in the UK, Netherlands, Thailand, Chile, Canada, Spain, Italy, France, Philippines, Sweden, Belgium, Mexico, and Australia/New Zealand. In 2015, Barbato and Bailey's production company World of Wonder launched RuPaul's DragCon, a massive convention that celebrates (and sells) all things drag. The convention, taking place annually in Los Angeles, New York, and London, has grown from 14,000 to 50,000 attendees, and witnesses up to $5.63 million in revenue from ticket sales, merchandise, vendor booths, special events, signings, and meet-and-greets.[106]

Atop all this are RuPaul's many products that she markets on and off the show: her own candy bar, a perfume and cosmetics line, and multiple music albums.[107] RuPaul has also developed spin-offs to the regular *Drag Race* format including *Secret Celebrity Drag Race* and *Drag U* in which former *Drag Race* contestants provide drag makeovers to celebrities and everyday people, respectively. And before I forget, there's her podcast *What's the Tee?* that she hosts with *Drag Race* resident judge and long-time friend Michelle Visage, and her Netflix original narrative series *AJ and the Queen*.

The scope of her empire is dizzying, but I'm not done yet.

In addition to all RuPaul's own merchandise and media products are the many business ventures she and the show have spawned. Queer bars screen the show at weekly watch parties, hiring local drag queens, or even flying in queens from the show, to headline the night.[108] Al and Chuck Travel offers pricey gay cruises that feature *Drag Race* alumni lip-synching, doing stand-up comedy, and mingling with guests. New web-based drag reality competitions have been inspired by the show, such as Mexico's "Las Mas Dragas," the campy "Camp Wannakiki," and the spooky "Dragula." Drag queen BibleGirl launched her website Dragqueenmerch. com in 2014 as a venue for drag artists to sell their own likeness on t-shirts and other products; by 2017 the company grossed over one million dollars.[109] Cosmetics companies such as Sugarpill collaborate with show contestants to release lipsticks or eyeshadows named after them that then become their best-selling products.[110]

BibleGirl and Sugarpill of course have booths at DragCon, as do as do the many small businesses now catering to drag amateurs and fans with: prosthetic breast plates; t-shirts with sassy quotes; extravagant pageant-style jewelry; and bamboo hand fans with fabulous prints and slogans. These vendors appeal to drag artists, amateurs, and fans seeking to emulate the expensive aesthetics of the TV show; drag queens might spend anywhere from $300 to $2500 on a look.[111] But the vendors at DragCon and that orbit around *Drag Race* actually appeal to an even more lucrative audience: tweens and teenage girls.

NeolibRulism: Economy, Individuality, and the Inner Saboteur

RuPaul is regularly asked whether she sees drag going mainstream as a threat to its critical edge. In one interview she responds, "There are the people who understand that this [fame] is a matrix . . . and then there are people who buy it lock, stock, and barrel . . . drag breaks the fourth wall."[112] She says elsewhere, "I've always seen behind the curtain. I've always seen that the guy controlling the buttons, that's the Wiz. I've always been able to see that the emperor is wearing no clothes."[113] RuPaul's quotes make me bristle because she herself is so complicit in obscuring the operations of the "matrix" by hiding behind the curtain.

Take for example the drag transformation. It's a very common trope in film, TV, and photography to capture drag artists in front of mirrors as they get ready, gluing on eyelashes and facial hair. But RuPaul is rarely ever shown in the process of getting ready, and her drag transformation by a team of stylists is infamously secretive. In obscuring process, she renders drag a kind of "complete" gender transformation. Further, from the show's inception to the present, RuPaul and her judges have repeatedly criticized contestants for not investing enough in this project of "illusion" when their penis-tuck is not pulled back enough, their hips are not wide enough to create an hourglass figure that balances wide shoulders, or their "boy hair" or hip pads are showing: "I still see 'boy'!" she says.

RuPaul has said that drag's subversive nature will keep it from mainstream co-optation. However, she purports that drag is only subversive when cisgender men confound gender hegemony through "illusion," performing as women. For the first eight years of the US version, trans queens were not invited to compete on the show even though they make up a significant and valuable contingent of the drag scene. The deliberate exclusion of trans women is a way of insisting that gender crossing and illusion *is* the art form. This subscribes to colonial logics described in Chapters 1 and 2 that require stark differentiation between male and female, men and women. The boy-to-girl transformation lauded by the show excludes not only trans women but people of many *other* genders. Through 2019, the audition process required you to film in both your "boy drag" and performance looks; the wording has now changed to "out of drag." RuPaul's public comments and the show's gendered expectations have gotten the drag mogul in hot water, and several trans alumni from the show have called out her transphobia.

The show has shifted its language in response; for example, instead of announcing "Gentlemen, start your engines. And may the best woman, win!" RuPaul now announces, "Racers, start your engines. And may the best drag queen win!" The show and its franchises have, in recent years, also featured trans women, a trans man, and a cis woman, as well as two-spirit and non-binary people. And yet RuPaul conforms to, and sells, colonial logics of binary gender by performing, subscribing to, or even insisting on idealized forms of female embodiment. This has shifted and changed a bit over time. On different franchises of the show, where the judging panel and drag scene are different, or the competitive stakes are lower, other gender configurations are possible: *Drag Race UK* featured a queen who kept her chest and armpit hair visible, *Drag Race Holland* included a bearded queen, and *Secret Celebrity Drag Race* starred cis women performing in feminine *and* masculine drag. But these moves look new and progressive *only because* the production house instituted and aggressively policed definitions of drag for over a decade.

I am genuinely a BIG fan of the show, and I admire the platform it has provided to drag as an art and cultural practice. I've watched the seasons several times over, and not simply to write this book. I'm absolutely one of those gays who has a *Drag Race* quote for every occasion! Sickening, no? But I worry that the show has created a universe crafted around RuPaul herself and not the community-based work of drag. Frankly, RuPaul engages in forms of capitalist accumulation that decimate collectivity, uplift individuality, and reinscribe whiteness. On and off the show, she spouts a rhetoric that espouses radical individualism, one that pays little attention to systemic and social barriers to mobility.

RuPaul's discourse of individual uplift, her acquisition of fame, money, and influence, and her obfuscation of the collective work of drag operate in distinctly neoliberal logics, or (because we know she loves a pun) neolibRulism.

Neoliberalism's preference for free markets monetizes freedom as a feeling, turning feminist, Black, and queer struggles into sellable slogans. It also stitches the economic ethic of choice and free will into a cultural ethos of individual responsibility, and we hear this in RuPaul's obsession with pop psychology on the show, encouraging competitors to confront their "inner saboteur," rather than forms of structural inequity.

There is certainly a redistributive ethic to *RuPaul's Drag Race*. The moment a new lineup of queens is announced, they are instantly booked for shows nationwide if not internationally, and their Instagram followings multiply by the thousands. You'll notice though that white queens are much more likely to reach a million followers on Instagram than their Black and Brown counterparts. But as RuPaul initiates a future of fame for the queens invited on to her show, she and World of Wonder production house do little to prepare them for the grueling labor market they are about to enter. Having survived homelessness and earning gig-to-gig, she certainly knows that a career in drag is a hustle; and yet she does little to scaffold the careers of the show's competitors, or create the conditions for a comfortable future.

Instead, she demands that the drag queens on her show do not spoil her name, or more specifically her brand. In January of 2020, "RuPaul's Drag Race LIVE!" opened in Las Vegas, an opulent revue featuring popular cast members from several seasons of the show. On the docuseries *RuPaul's Drag Race: Vegas Revue* we witness RuPaul attending a dress rehearsal for the debut show; rather than empathize with the body-breaking labor the queens are engaging in, she insists that they buck up and fix the show because it has her name on it. In the wake of competing on the show, the "dolls," as RuPaul calls them, face exhaustion, injuries, bills, unwieldy taxes, irregular travel schedules, lack of health care, and sleeplessness as they acquire fame beyond their towns and enter the global market.[114] Veteran contestant Silky Nutmeg Ganache called out the show producer's lack of care for the performers post-filming. In the wake of abuse she experienced on social media as a fat, Black drag queen, she pointed how the show benefits financially from contestant's on-screen antics, but does little to protect them from audience threats or offer them mental health care.[115]

Several performers from *Drag Race* have been screwed over by agents and venues alike, and two former contestants, Shangela and Latrice Royale, have started their own management firms to represent fellow queens and prevent the loss of work and money.[116] Shangela and Latrice's labor is much more in line with the drag economies I've been a part of in Chicago, Texas, and Boston. Queens regularly work for other queens. They provide expertise for and even barter with each other when official businesses don't exist or are too expensive, be it wig-styling, gown-sewing, hip-pad carving, sound mixing, etc. Drag artists curate their own shows to lift up Black and Brown performers when they see that mainstream gay bars tokenize drag queens of color, or don't include drag kings or genderfuck artists.

The uneven market for performers of color was especially apparent in Chicago's drag scene and this came to a head in the Summer of 2020. As the Movement for Black Lives was reignited following the murder of

George Floyd in Minneapolis, reckonings around systemic anti-Blackness arose in companies and industries across the US and world. Shea Coulée, winner of *All Stars* Season 5, spoke up at a Black Lives Matter rally in Chicago's Boystown neighborhood about the anti-Black racism she, other performers, and poor Black youth experienced in the area. This is a complaint I'd heard from Shea well before her appearance on *Drag Race*, when she visited a class I was teaching at Northwestern University in 2014. She told my students that clubs wanted Black queer and trans people to be fabulous queens on stage, but didn't welcome them as patrons, and even questioned their presence in the neighborhood as they walked from the train to the club.

Following Shea's and others' powerful callout at the rally, a collective of Black queer and trans folks held a virtual town hall that made clear to white nightlife producers and bar owners/managers the racism and classism they enforced. For example, one influential nightlife producer required that performers she booked not repeat the same wigs or outfits on her stage, placing pressure on artists to spend more money than they were earning. Other *Drag Race* queens like Bob the Drag Queen and Peppermint were co-hosts of a two-day nationwide virtual Black Queer Town Hall in the summer of 2020 that mapped the many systemic and social crises facing Black queer and trans people.

Bob, Shea, and Peppermint use their fame to reframe national and regional dialogues around race and power. RuPaul shows little investment in this kind of collective work, as if she assumes that the show's presence is *doing* enough. Other than encouraging voting during national elections, little of her message is about transforming systems, and most of her catchphrases are about individuality and choice: Everybody say love; If you can't love yourself, how in the hell are you gonna love somebody else? We as gay people, we get to choose our families! She doesn't make clear the distinction between getting to and *having to* choose families in the face of transphobia and homophobia.

As the show has progressed, RuPaul has embraced the role of a self-help figure, attempting to unlock the queens' potential through one-on-one consultations as they get ready for challenges. RuPaul regularly invites the performers to confront and overcome their "inner saboteur," that inner self that keeps telling them, "You can't do this. You don't deserve this."

RuPaul uses her own narrative of making it out of the projects as a poor Black child to suggest that one's past can be overcome. A Season Ten challenge

asks contestants to present two different looks on the
runway, one as their queenly persona and the other as
their evil twin modeled around their inner saboteur.
In a rare moment, RuPaul models the task at hand. As
she talks to the queens in the workroom dressed in signature Klein Epstein and Parker bespoke printed suit,
her inner saboteur enters to interrupt. This evil twin
is wearing a red track suit, sandals, and a neon blonde
wig (not the more natural blondes queen RuPaul wears
on the stage). The inner saboteur walks with a slouch-
ing swagger and speaks in African American vernac-
ular English. RuPaul's saboteur is a Black-er, poorer,
lazier, more "hood" version of herself. The fantasy of
whiteness, wealth, and gender conformity is not the
inner saboteur, one that made her younger self feel marginalized and excluded. Rather this fantasy is set up as
the desired future that the poor Black saboteur is in the
way of. There's a way we could understand the inner
saboteur as experiences of anti-Blackness, homophobia, and class-bias as they settle into the body and mind.
But RuPaul turns that structural inequity into a personal, individual insecurity that one needs to overcome.
I really would have thought that Ru's inner saboteur
might have been a white man in a business suit telling her
everything she, and other Black queer people, are not.

Certainly my inner saboteur is that white man at *Jai Ho!* telling my student I'm not a real drag queen.

We know that psyches too are colonized,[117] and I'm not suggesting that there aren't hurdles such as imposter syndrome or internalized homophobia and transphobia that affect queer, trans, and people of color's success on the show. But RuPaul's insistence on the contestant's personal responsibility to overcome their racial, classed, or regional origins relies on the neoliberal language of individualism.[118] Rather than suggesting that these barriers should never have impinged on their psyche in the first place, that the saboteur is cis-hetero patriarchal racial capitalism, that the saboteur is the system, RuPaul insists that *the queens* must change, *not* the competition, judging rubrics, society, or institutions.

In 2018, RuPaul published a book titled *GuRu*—an excellent pun!—cultivating a whole persona around individual betterment. Leading up to this publication were RuPaul's keynote presentations at DragCon. In 2015, RuPaul lectured about the value of LGBT history, the transfer of legacies of struggle across generations, and the Black and queer blood that was "spilled" to make such a gathering of outsiders, freaks, and weirdos possible.[119] But her keynote shifts tone in 2016: "Ru does not present himself, like he did the previous year, as a queer knowledge keeper. This year, he performs a type of 'self-help guRu' role who wants to give the audience life advice."[120] And while we'd expect a more politicized voice at DragCon 2017 following the election of Donald Trump and the rollback of immigrant and trans rights, RuPaul keeps to her self-help rhetoric, instructing audience members to "clear out the blockage" in themselves.[121]

RuPaul's investment in neoliberalism is evident not only in her psychobabble, but also in her firestorm of products, show franchises, and events described in the previous section. And of course, there is her infamous fracking reveal. In May 2020, RuPaul stated in an NPR interview that she leases mineral and water rights on her 60,000 acre ranch in Wyoming to oil companies. Social media users, activists, and journalists used this information to determine that these companies are engaged in fracking on RuPaul's land; fracking is a process of oil mining that severely depletes land and creates excessive and dangerous waste.[122] This form of settler capitalist extraction wreaks havoc by upsetting ecosystems, releasing lethal gases, igniting fires, improperly disposing of waste, building pipelines through Indigenous territory, and destroying buried Native artifacts. It renders land unlivable.

RuPaul's "empire" extends not simply to the drag shows, queens, and products she presides over, but also extractive landowning practices.

A contemporary of RuPaul's, Linda Simpson offers a valuable commentary that suggests that though RuPaul may be mainstream, drag is not: "it's telling that the top person of the genre has been the same since 1992. Drag is still a ghetto. The entertainment industry is still unsure what to do with drag . . . Not to unseat Ru, but is there room for other sensibilities?"[123] I think Linda Simpson is right about the media's excitement for RuPaul; the rainbow ceiling remains largely undisturbed as long as there's a single figure we can prop up as the sparkling example of queer mobility. RuPaul, caught in the mirage of fame, doesn't see the matrix at work. *She* moves into the mainstream and her show acquires recognition and ratings, yet these are a meager concession to LGBTQ people's demand for visibility, representation, safety, and life. The celebration of her singular excellence creates pomp and flash that obscures the daily violence endured by Black trans women, sex workers, and gender-nonconforming people.

Indeed, in abandoning her androgynous and hooker personas for a much more cis-passing glamorous style, she too rhinestones over systemic barriers to safety, health, wealth, and beauty.

Representing Race on *RuPaul's Drag Race*

Season 11 and 12 of *RuPaul's Drag Race* both featured Muslim contestants. On Season 11, Muslim Kenyan migrant Mercedes Iman Diamond is wary about discussing her religion with her co-stars, anxious about the stereotypes they might harbor. Her—spoiler alert— very short narrative arc on the show sees her announcing at her elimination, "I am ready to show the world, Muslim is not a terrorist." The producers take a tokenistic approach to her appearance on the show; the uniqueness of her storyline must come from her Muslim-ness because, well, an African immigrant already won the first season of *Drag Race*.

Jackie Cox, a favorite on Season 12, talks about her Iranian heritage, her fondness for hearing Farsi spoken on *I Dream of Jeannie*, and the detachment she feels as a diasporic subject from Iran because of the Muslim government's homophobia. Though she is not religious, Jackie, who passes for white and often nods to sixties camp tropes in her style, insists on her Iranian and Muslim identities as distinguishing elements of her stage persona. She always greets RuPaul by saying, "Salaam RuPaul joon."

In a runway themed "Stars and Stripes Forever," Jackie walks the ramp in a silver and red striped caftan, with a blue hijab stamped with silver stars—an especially modest look for the fabulous stage. One of the guest judges that day is veteran actor Jeff Goldblum; he asks Jackie during the feedback session: "Are you religious, may I ask? . . . isn't this an interesting wrinkle though? Is there something in that religion [Islam] that is anti-homosexuality and anti-woman? Does that complicate the issue?" Goldblum is drawing on the insidious rhetoric of empire-building that positions the US as an exceptionally feminist and queer nation in relation to the supposedly repressive Muslim world when he suggests that Islam, queerness, femininity, and America are together incompatible, a "wrinkle" in Jackie's patriotic ensemble as it were.[124] Whether in Goldblum's Islamophobic engagement with Jackie Cox or the reductive storyline given to Mercedes Iman Diamond, *RuPaul's Drag Race* boxes queens from minoritized racial, ethnic, and religious backgrounds into quite limiting modes of representation predicated on colonial and racist stereotypes.[125]

RuPaul's Drag Race is the veritable gateway drug into The RuPaul Industrial Complex. The runway features fantastic fashions, the "lip-synch for your life" battles are thrilling, the comedic timing and puns will make your belly hurt from laughter, the show is filled with sheer excellence, excellence that has been plucked from small gay stages across the US on to national and global television. For all the offerings it makes as a ground-breaking show, critics of *RuPaul's Drag Race* have shown that the series props up US exceptionalism, fatphobia, classism, transphobia, and misogyny.[126]

In the way the show configures race and Indigeneity, it is clear that the labor and artistry of people of color are managed differently from white people. Diversity on the show is highly contrived. Various cadres of drag—cabaret, fashion, comedy, pageant, Ballroom— are included, but drag kings and genderfuck performers never make the cut. There is always mixed racial representation, but only in limited numbers: with few exceptions, there is only one queen from Puerto Rico and only one Asian American queen per season.

We should be skeptical of this curated inclusion of diasporic artists because it allows the show to manufacture US exceptionalism, that the US is unique in its acceptance of various kinds of marginalized people.

By repeatedly asking the queens to perform their patriotism, the US is propped up as a welcoming nation

where gender freaks can find refuge from homophobic elsewheres.[127] Performances of US patriotism are
regularly scripted into the show: Season 3 contestants
were asked to make a video in support of US troops
abroad, a riff on the 40s-pinup girl entertaining army
men; on season 5, military veterans were made over
into drag queens; over several seasons contestants have
had to dance and lip-synch to RuPaul's original song
"I Am American"; and on seasons 4, 8, and 12 (aired in
election years) RuPaul has held mock elections for the
"Next Drag President of the United States." These performances of patriotism stand in tension with the ways
that the Muslim world is staged through Mercedes Iman
Diamond and Jackie Cox. The tropes through which
they become sympathetic rely on the US being seen
as a site of refuge from a sexually regressive/repressive
Islamic world. What never gets portrayed, on *Drag Race*
or elsewhere, are the abundant and vibrant forms of
gender and sexual dissidence that flourish, sometimes
in the open and sometimes underground, in majority
Muslim countries.

These hyper-representational strategies affect many
queens of color. Asian queens find themselves having
to perform forms of Asianness that don't correspond to
their own ethnic heritage simply to be legible *as* Asian,

to read in ways the audience and judges might find familiar and entertaining.[128] Season 8's Kim Chi is often commended for the many ways she broke the national, racial, ethnic mold, by referencing couture designers in her runway looks and critiquing anti-Asian bias in the gay community.[129]

And yet the show finds other ways to script her into a narrative of rescue from repressive Asianness. Kim Chi, a first-generation Korean American from Chicago, reveals matter-of-factly that she is not out to her mother. While it is a non-issue for Kim Chi, RuPaul makes quite a deal of it! To the other judges RuPaul remarks that "When her mother gets to meet her [in her drag avatar], Kim Chi will fully blossom." Not only is this in line with RuPaul's penchant for pop psychology, it positions coming out of the closet as the proper destination for all LGBT people *and* their families. On that same episode, guest judge David Sedaris describes Kim Chi's portrayal of her mother as "closeted culturally," suggesting that Korean culture is repressive. At the live finale, recorded after all the other episodes had aired, RuPaul asks Kim Chi if she has finally come out to her mother. Hearing that she has not, RuPaul insists that after the show they go together to Chicago to come out to Kim Chi's mom. This thread on the show, that Kim Chi is artistically or emotionally stuck because she hasn't fully "come out" replicates discourses that pathologize people of color for not conforming to white ways of doing gender and sexuality. It allows figures like RuPaul, as a stand in for mainstream US gayness, to position themselves as paternalistic heroes by bringing freedom to people they think are oppressed by their culture's "inherent" homophobia.[130]

As early as Season Three, we see patterns emerge on the show that require Latinx, Asian, Indigenous, and Black queens to perform racial authenticity far differently from their white counterparts. In this season, Latina queens Alexis Mateo and Yara Sofia are praised for showing "personality" when they perform in ways that reveal their Puerto Ricanness, when they are "cha cha" or "flirtatious."[131] "Personality" is a deracinated word that stands in for the excessive performances assumed to be authentic to these Latina artists, as if "Show us your personality" means "Show us who you really are," which in turn means, "Be your race/culture."

Similarly, Stacy Layne Matthews, a fat, rural Native American (Lumbee) queen is praised when she performs a Southern Black accent and eats fried chicken on screen. Where there aren't easy Native stereotypes for Stacy to tap into on a show like this, by performing

Black stereotypes, Stacy appeals to the judges' demand for "personality."[132] But even when queens aren't performing racial authenticity, the show teaches us to see them through a racialized lens. When light-skinned Latina queens walk the runway in sequined and rhinestoned gowns, the judges regularly make a reference to the American Latino Media Awards (ALMA). While their gowns may be as opulent as their white peers' on the same runway, Latinas are imagined to be walking a completely different red carpet.

A few queens on the show have named their Indigenous heritage: Stacy Layne Matthews (Lumbee) on Season Three, Shuga Cain (Apache) on Season Eleven, Sasha Colby (Kānaka Maoli) winner of Season Fourteen, Ilona Verley (Nlaka'pamux) on Season One of *Canada's Drag Race*, Jojo Zaho (Biripi and Worimi) on Season One of *Drag Race Down Under*, and Inti (Quechua) on Season One of *Drag Race España*. The winner of Stacy's season was Raja, a Southeast Asian queen who, when invited to walk in an "all-American" themed runway, sported a Native American chief's feathered headdress while RuPaul complimented her, saying, "Can you get more American than Native American?" That Raja's appropriative gesture is applauded as fashion-forward on a season that features the show's first Native contestant is uncomfortable. But the show moreover sets up Raja and Stacy as oppositional figures: "The clash between Stacy's 'country-ness' and Raja's cosmopolitan-ness is striking. While Stacy is from a small town and not a high-fashion queen, Raja's 'I travel a lot more than most' status allows her to claim avant-garde fashion."[133] Following the show's rhetoric, Indigenous bodies are fixed as regional, immobile, and un-urban, even while indigeneity (headdress, costume, and jewelry) circulates to make settler Asian bodies fabulous, and to give them (aesthetic) claims to land.[134]

A regular event on the show is the "makeover" challenge, in which people who don't do drag get to be dolled up in the signature aesthetic of the queen they are paired with. On Season One of *Canada's Drag Race* this challenge invited beneficiaries of the Rainbow Railroad to be put into drag. Rainbow Railroad is a not-for-profit organization that secures asylum in Canada for LGBTQ people facing persecution in their home countries. Asylum can save the lives of individuals who have been persecuted, or fear persecution, in their home country. However, the bureaucratic and clunky asylum process requires asylees, experts, and lawyers to testify that the origin country is unequivocally sexist/homophobic/

transphobic, setting up the receiving country as exceptionally hospitable.[135]

On this episode of *Drag Race*, the Rainbow Railroad
guests name both their gratitude for Canada's embrace,
as well as the fears that drove them out of Jamaica, Syria,
Indonesia, and Uganda. Being able to do drag, to be
publicly effeminate on global television, becomes a way
of exhibiting Canadian exceptionalism. But the stories that asylees must narrate, whether in immigration
proceedings or on TV, are always more complicated
and textured. The Indonesian guest mentions how he
could be killed for doing drag back home. But across
the archipelago there are vibrant drag, transgender, and
waria performance cultures, whether in Hindu Bali or
Muslim Jakarta, that are painted over by the show's sim-
plistic representation. I'm not saying this to mitigate
the Indonesian asylee's need for refuge, but instead to
nuance this hyperbolic narrative of his home country
that he has to perform in order to secure asylum and to
comfort Canadians (who are themselves settlers!) who
might question his migration.

To justify migration into tightly closed western borders, people from the global south are expected to spin
horrific stories about their homelands, and must even get
scholars and experts to testify that the nation is, without

question, homophobic or transphobic. To be legible as vulnerable migrants, LGBT asylees can't simply explain the individualized conditions they may be fleeing: conservative families, corrupt leadership in their village, extortion from neighborhood police. Asylum processes notoriously require them to foreclose *all* possibilities of queerness in the home nation, to demonize the home nation. This turns the receiving nation into a progressive and generous benefactor, reproducing the kind of Western exceptionalism that is used to justify violent incursions into other parts of the world in service of liberating gender and sexuality. This narrative of Canada's acceptance of queer migrants, part of its state-sanctioned multiculturalism,[136] obscures the ongoing violence against trans and two-spirit Indigenous folks and anti-Black racism that remains unreckoned with.

In the final episode of that season, First Nations two-spirit contestant Ilona Verley responds directly to this invisibility and silence. They step on the show's catwalk wearing an outfit that incorporates eagle feathers, fringe, jingles, and ribbons that all signify their Nlaka'pamux heritage. They hold their red-gloved hand over their mouth. Through this gesture they cite the logo of the movement for Missing and Murdered Indigenous Women, a red handprint that activists often paint over their mouths. The precarity of Indigenous women's life is part of the ongoing settlement of Canadian territories that includes sexual and epistemic violence that affects trans and two-spirit people like Ilona. Their grandmother is a residential school survivor, and because these reform programs stripped their grandmother of access to First Nations cultures, it took longer for Ilona to learn about two-spirit identities.[137] Ilona's story is a valuable reminder of the ways that colonialism has eliminated gender variance, and how drag, even on the mainstream venue of *Drag Race*, offers a response to historical and ongoing processes of colonial violence.

RuPaul's Drag Race and its infamous host reproduce notions of beauty, success, and professionalism that skew toward whiteness, binary gender, and individualism. However, queens like Shea Coulée, Ilona Verley, Peppermint, and Bob the Drag Queen use their fame to call for justice well beyond their individual traumas and beyond LGBTQ issues alone. Angele Anang, winner of *Drag Race Thailand* Season Two, also uses her platform to call out the privileging of light skin in Thai notions of beauty, and to make room for trans women in the drag scene.

These *Drag Race* queens may be an exception to Ru, but they are not the exception to the Ru-le. Drag artists regularly use their craft to stage critiques of colonialism and to imagine other modes of being in their body that navigate, resist, and escape imperialist logics. Once this book is out, LaWhore will likely never make it on *Drag Race*! So while I give up *my* dreams of fame, let me give publicity to a slew of other artists whose drag deserves to be celebrated for the brilliance with which they respond to histories of colonialism, simultaneously imagining other worlds full of pleasure and fun.

Chapter 4

DECOLONIZATION AT THE CLUB: STAGING VIOLENCE, EMBODYING PLEASURE IN DRAG

Fugitive Nights

In the summer of 2019, the Berlin Nightclub in Chicago launched *Mom Jeans*, a new monthly drag show featuring Chanel Mercedes-Benz, Irregular Girl, and K'hole Kardashian performing "your favorite white anthems!" Berlin was one of my favorite queer clubs when I lived in Chicago, especially because of their edgy and creative programming. I'd left in 2014, and I was excited to return and relive my hipster gay days in this grungy bar. The inaugural *Mom Jeans* show lampooned whiteness: the high-waisted, loose-legged jeans known as "mom jeans," the rowdy and lowbrow stylings of restaurateur and food-show host Guy Fieri, and a taste-test competition featuring blindfolded audience members trying to distinguish between "white" seasonings like mayonnaise and lemon-pepper.

Identifying "white culture" is a well-worn path, made popular by the blog-turned-book *Stuff White People Like*, that leads quickly from avocado toast to colonialism. *Stuff White People Like* began as a blog in 2008 with individual entries such as Sea Salt, Hummus, and Recycling. It satirized North American white folks whose liberal politics suggested anti-racist attitudes, but who implicitly secured their privilege through seemingly innocuous consumption practices. It was humorous for Berlin to host a show like this, since the club is known for avant-garde but not necessarily political drag. In its ironic whiteness, *Mom Jeans* could easily have been apolitical, much like *Stuff White People Like* has become with the book version now sold in Urban Outfitters stores. It was far from it . . .

As the emcee announced that the cast only performed songs by white people, I shuddered at what fuckery I might be in store for. Cue Kelly Clarkson's "Breakaway." Chanel Mercedes-Benz, a Black queen in a dowdy skirt and headscarf—no sequins, no glitter—dawdled in, holding a branch bearing tufts of cotton. Uh oh! For every dollar tip someone handed her, she handed them a piece of cotton and bowed—the obedient slave. I was mortified, but also stifling giggles. The Kelly Clarkson fans reading this know how the song goes: "Take a risk / Take a chance / Make a change / And breakaaaaaaway." Chanel flung the branch, grabbed her baby—where the prop even came from remains a mystery—and started running in place. We screamed with laughter as this song about individual white-lady self-empowerment suddenly turned into a fugitive slave anthem. Our screams only amplified when Chanel pulled her lover from the audience, a Black man, barefoot, in dark slacks, loose tank top, and messily styled hair. He picked up her dollar tips from the floor as she continued to lip-synch. She pocketed the money, grabbed his hand, and baby in bosom, led them all to freedom through the crowd, into the darkness of the club. No final bow, no fabulous dress reveal, just freedom.

I wasn't expecting to witness an escape from enslavement in the nightclub on a random Monday night. But this is what drag can do. Audiences turn to the stage to witness something beyond our present moment. While we stand there sipping vodka sodas, we are suddenly dragged through time, into impossible futures and fugitive pasts.

It was a reminder of drag's potential for reconnecting with radical Black histories. In the late nineteenth century, former slave William Dorsey Swann, who referred to himself as "The Queen," was arrested along with several other Black men in Washington, D.C., on suspicion of running a brothel. Swann was amongst a cohort of Black men who enjoyed dolling themselves up in fancy feminine styles, and gathering at "balls," which police purposefully misinterpreted as brothels and in turn raided.[138] Chanel Mercedes-Benz's scene of Black fugitivity took me by surprise at Berlin Nightclub. But when I think about Swann's story I'm reminded that drag is part of a larger story about the pleasures of performance, and its relationship to the policing of Black people in the Americas.

Like Chanel Mercedes-Benz's masterful rescripting of "Breakaway," many drag performances make apparent the legacies of colonialism that bear on the performer's body while also inviting us to laugh, cheer, and dance. This chapter is about performances that speak directly to some of the mechanisms of colonialism: orientalism, incarceration, criminalization, racial capitalism, and displacement. These are well-worn topics for academia and activism, but are rarely imagined as the provenance of the nightclub! These performances engage explicitly with history, violence, economy, and activism, and you'll see that drag is simultaneously playful as it is political or painful. Much like in Chapter 2, I want to offer my readers ways to witness drag differently, to see that gender is not the only project of the art form. When we divert the discerning eye that is invested only in gender transformation, we can see the *other* issues and concepts that drag artists are trying to stage.

Settler Colonialism

When colonizers turn Indigenous people's land into property—through corrupt treaties, manipulations of law, violent incursion, and genocide—they simultaneously displace Indigenous people, and conjure their own "right" to that land. But some drag artists use performance as opportunity to critique the occupation of Indigenous land, and to reimagine the borders drawn and policed in service of settler colonialism. For example, Arouse Falastin, also known as the Bride of Palestine, is a Palestinian artist with Israeli citizenship. She lip synchs to songs that lay claim to nation, such as the Lebanese "Safwa Naqba, We Will Stay," but also positions herself as the Bride—on the cusp of inclusion—in order to gesture to the ongoing and incomplete condition of becoming a nation/citizen, as well as the unfinished nature of gender and sexuality.[139] For Arouse, as well as Miss Chief and Papi Churro discussed below, gender, body, and land become interwoven.

Miss Chief Eagle Testickle (suggestively sounding like Mischief Egotistical) is the drag alter ego of Canadian Cree artist Kent Monkman. Miss Chief appears in Monkman's video and performance work, but she can also be found in his elaborate landscape paintings, posing sexily in her red thigh-high boots. In these

paintings, Miss Chief is variously having her dick sucked
by a white Royal Canadian Mountie or painting white
subjects in nature, turning the colonial landscape por-
trait on its head—pun intended. Monkman's paintings
reimagine the landscapes rendered by colonial artists
who emptied land of the Indigenous people that they
had killed or enslaved. Further, he reinscribes two-spirit
people back into Indigenous gender and sexual matrices
and considers their relationship to colonial encounter.
Miss Chief's drag escorts us through time to feel gender
and colonization again and differently.

In the short film titled "Mary" (2011), Monkman
simultaneously stages the encounter between Indigenous
peoples and the British crown (specifically the 1860 visit
to Montreal by the Prince of Wales), and reflects on the
legacies of Christianity as a device of colonialism drawing on the trope of Mary Magdalene washing the feet
of Jesus Christ. This Christian imagery reminds us that
religion was a particularly violent force of settler colonialism, especially in the form of Residential Schools,
which stripped First Nations, Metis, and Inuit people
from their culture, language, and communities in the
name of evangelism.

Monkman reenacts the colonial encounter through a
foot fetish scene, one in which the contract of mutuality

is broken. Miss Chief Eagle Testickle walks confidently up to the figure sitting on a throne who is dressed like European royalty. She kneels in front of him and looks up into his eyes as her hair catches the wind. Confident but submissive in a slutty red outfit—fuck-me pleather knee-high boots, strappy sequin dress, gloves, satin choker—she removes the shoes and then socks from the man's foot. He licks his lips and strokes the arm handle, anticipating the sexual pleasure of Miss Chief's foot worship as she brings the bare white foot to her cheek.

But when oil-black tears trickle from her eyes on to the pale white foot, his (and the scene's) eroticism is cut by discomfort. The oil-tears signify the harm done by turning land into commodity—Canada's massive oil and gas industry not only intrudes into First Nations territories, but poisons that land and renders it unlivable. Text appears over the video, "We had an agreement," then "I agreed to share, not to surrender," and finally "How could you break your promise?" Fetish sex, often based on contracts of safety and mutual agreement, can turn power difference into pleasure play.[140] But Miss Chief's tears of black oil make clear that trust has been broken, that the land has been ravaged for extractive purposes. Through this image, she recalls the violation of colonial treaties under which land was seized and depleted instead of shared. Monkman uses drag aesthetics as a venue to stage the colonial violation of consent and contracts, both on feminine and queer bodies, and on land. The sequined dress, wind fan, and thigh-high boots keep us squarely in the nightlife aesthetics of drag, and the kneeling foot-fetish gesture locates us in queer sexual subcultures. In this way, the artist implicates gay white men and other subcultural queers, minoritarian subjects who *could* be allies in anti-colonial work, in the project of settlement as well.

Like Monkman, California-based drag king Papi Churro engages with the legacies of land occupation. In a 2020 video he made for web-streaming when living in Austin, Texas, Papi considers the multiple claims to space that people of color and Indigenous people make in a settler colonial state. At the beginning of the video, protestors walk and bike through Austin's downtown with Black Lives Matters signs chanting, "Whose streets?" "Our streets!" (Could this be the protest that interrupted LaWhore and friends!?) This footage is overlaid with Papi, refracted into three avatars, dancing and turning ritualistically one way and then another. The drums get louder, and then transition into the reverberations of an electric guitar. Papi's image becomes clear as the protest footage fades out. He is wearing a headdress made of feathers that ripple with gold and blue iridescence, colors that recall his Mayan and Aztec ancestry. There are skulls on his waist, and his face is painted in dark and light blues.

Papi lip-synchs to a metal song called "Mexica" by electronic rock duo Prayers. The vocalist sings about proudly claiming "Mexica," instead of "Hispano" and "Latino," as an identity that precedes the conquer and enslavement of Indigenous people by militarism and evangelism. Papi's Native dress, wide-open eyes, gnashing teeth, eyes rolling into his head, fire and smoke waving across his body may suggest a kind of primitivism. But the song's heavy metal sound, as well as the rock-goth aesthetic Papi is known for, diffuses a primitivist reading and manifests contemporary angst instead. His use of Indigenous imagery and spirituality could make the content difficult to interpret for a non-Indigenous audience, that kind of "I don't understand, this isn't for me, so I won't engage" or even "he's just performing his culture." But Papi works in multiple registers, combining ritual practice and heavy metal, to make legible his anger about settler histories. Anyone who's heard metal or rock before can tap into the resistant ideologies of this performance. Using the headbanging repetition of "Mexica, Mexica," Papi creates a fabulously monstrous

Indigenous body that refuses the civilizing projects of European colonization and instead describes the pyramids his people built.

Papi's choice of song is meaningful not only for its lyrics and genre but because the lead singer of Prayers is queer and undocumented. Layering Black Lives Matter's claim to the street, over Indigenous people's historic claims to land, over the militarized securitization of the US border that renders people undocumented, Papi shows settler colonialism to be an ongoing project working to disempower and eradicate Indigenous people.[141] Papi described to me how his Native heritage is made invisible by Latinidad, that people do not believe his Native heritage, even though his family carries the oral histories of enslavement and trafficking that displaced them. The song's use of English and Spanish simultaneously evidences colonialism's legacy and speaks against the entrapment these languages create. The unrelenting chant of "Mexica! Mexica!" suggests another language, another place, is possible. Through call and response, "Mexica! Mexica!" summons a decolonial future.

Orientalism

One way of exercising colonial control has been to create representations of the subordinated Other, images that suggest that they are knowable, static, and study-able. Orientalism is one of these knowledge projects, through which white artists, scholars, and traders have flattened "the East" into geishas, harems, spices, minarets and other such stereotypical formations. These visions have been used to feminize other nations, and justify colonization (see Chapter 2).

But what happens when an Indigenous Hawai'an drag queen indulges in Orientalism? Hawai'ian/ Kanaka Maoli drag queen Cocoa Chandelier cites Pacific Indigenous imagery and histories through her dress, feathers, and regal posture. But in one 2008 performance, Cocoa draws on Bollywood, Bhangra, belly dance costume, and harem imagery in ways that might read as orientalist. The story Cocoa tells through this drag number is of an imprisoned woman, the harem girl, attempting to escape her fate. According to Indigenous studies scholar Stephanie Nohelani Teves we could on one hand read this as an appropriation of the subjugated Asian woman trope.[142] On the other, she asks us to consider what other strategies a Kanaka Maoli queen has to stage herself and her people's story of struggle without resorting to Native dress, or replaying the redundant representations that Native people are always bound by: "By embodying this performative realm—the so-called harem—Cocoa Chandelier may well be replicating Orientalism, but she may also be understood to be availing herself strategically of a space that cannot be penetrated by the Western gaze, a space that can be liberating for Natives, especially for Kanaka Maoli, who continue to be hypervisible subjects."[143] The hypervisibility of Kanaka Maoli performance such as Hula is especially apparent in Hawai'i's tourist economy—one fueled by the US's military settlement of the Islands—that is expected to display and make available Indigenous performance to a white gaze.[144] I find Teves's reading of Cocoa Chandelier's performance to be generous and helpful; it can be such a struggle to stage one's racialized body when the tropes become so stagnant and ineffective.

Cocoa's geographic location asks us to afford her some grace and think in more complex terms about cultural appropriation, particularly *between* colonized cultures. At the same time, white drag communities have a long history of indulging in orientalism. This includes "Scheherazade parties" in the early twentieth century, where gay white men adorned themselves in the gilded finery of the East in order to feel fabulous and feminine.[145] In the 1980s, famed white Australian fashion innovator Leigh Bowery amalgamated South Asian symbols and fashions in a series of infamous makeup and outfit combos for the nightclub that he titled "Pakis from Outer Space."[146] Bowery, who is renowned for popularizing genderfuck and tranimal drag, got to enjoy being on the cutting edge of fashion by donning South Asian styles in ways that many "Pakis" would be dismissed for because they were simply "performing their culture." More recently, white drag queens have performed the multi-armed Hindu goddess, danced to songs like "Firework" or "Tik Tok" dressed as suicide bombers (indicated by hijabs, bindis, and dynamite strapped their body), or worn adult diapers as bottom-wear in ode to Mahatma Gandhi.

The fascination with the gender and sexual alterity of "exotic" cultures is part of the process of colonization, in that it makes the objects and aesthetics of their culture knowable and acquirable. Given this recurring orientalism in the drag world, it's not uncommon to see Asian diasporic drag queens respond by parodying white fascinations with the East, especially through Madonna. In 1998, Madonna was in her orientalist phase—each of her albums captures some phase of her psycho-spiritual life—and released her excellent album *Ray of Light*. The tracks include a heavily Anglicized Sanskrit chant, and the various music videos feature henna-ed hands, kimonos, and geisha-inspired makeup. Asian American drag queens regularly send up Madonna's orientalism: at a 1999 South Asian performance evening in Manhattan, desi drag queens gyrated to "Shanti/Ashtangi,"[147] in 2010 LaWhore Vagistan did yoga on a club stage to the same song in Chicago, and in 2014 Asian American queen Chi-Chi Kago performed to "Shanti/Ashtangi" wrapped messily in sari-like fabrics at a Madonna tribute night in the Bay Area.[148] These parodic performances function as a commentary on the career and wealth she has built by appropriating queer, Black, Latinx, and Asian aesthetics.

In queer Asian communities, we often discuss how orientalism plays out through desire and dating.[149] Asian men are sometimes regarded as the submissive feminine Other to white men, and there are cultural phenomena built around this such as the terms "rice queen" (a white man who likes Asian men) and "rice bars" (nightclubs where white men go to pick up Asian lovers) or David Henry Hwang's play *M. Butterfly*. This trope was at the center of Miss Shu Mai's 2020 *Send Noodz* performance. *Send Noodz* is an Asian and Pacific Islander drag night hosted in Los Angeles. Miss Shu Mai, a Taiwanese-Hong Kongese drag queen appeared on stage with a long black wig, red cat-eye glasses, a leopard print short dress, and a pregnancy bump—she was the spitting image of Vietnamese-Chinese American comedian Ali Wong.

Miss Shu Mai lip-synched to Wong's shtick from her stand-up special *Hard Knock Wife*. Shu Mai's very precise routine recounts Wong's theorization of sex with white men; when they eat her out she gets to dominate the colonizer: "I'm absorbing all of that privilege, and all of that entitlement . . . also he's so vulnerable down there. I could just crush your head at any moment white man . . . Colonizer! Colonizer!" The music suddenly kicks in with the revving sounds that beckon Britney Spears's song "Womanizer." When the lyrics arrive, instead of Spears's sultry sound, we unexpectedly hear Miss Shu Mai's more masculine voice singing "Colonizer, colonizer, you're a colonizer baby!"[150]

Shu Mai is on the one hand a perfect Ali Wong, visually in costume and styling, and sonically because of her lip-synch. But when her own voice arrives to extend Wong's "Colonizer, colonizer" reprimand, it messes with gender and artistry. In a masculine, untrained voice, Shu Mai sings, "Boy I'm not your fetish, I know just what you are ah-ah / Don't ask me where I'm from, I know just what you are ah-ah . . . Pay reparations. Colonizer." With these lyrics, Shu Mai critiques the common exotification of Asian women and queers, and concretely aligns fetishization, exoticism, and orientalism with colonization.

As during Chanel Mercedes-Benz's enactment of
Black fugitivity in the club, I find myself shocked to
hear words like "colonizer" sung out loud in a bar. The
affirming screams and eager tipping by the audience in
response remind me that decolonial theory has a public and popular life even in nightlife settings. There is
a hunger for critiques of colonialism at the club! This
scenario is very much the heart of my first book, *Ishtyle:
Accenting Gay Indian Nightlife*—clubgoers and performers
are always engaged in political work, even when—or
precisely because—it looks like laughter, enthusiasm,
and fun!

The examples I've provided so far are drawn
from my engagement with Asian America and Asian
American studies. This is a scholarly field that has long
been under contestation. The term generally hails East
Asian people (Chinese, Japanese, Korean), and South
and Southeast Asians have pushed to be acknowledged
and included in the category. Further, Pacific Islanders
have called for a rethinking of the continental framing
of this term, broader consideration of US colonialism in
the Pacific, and the value of postcolonial, Indigenous,
and critical race critique together—think for example

of Teves's commentary on Hawai'ian orientalism above. Asian American studies has however been quite slow to reimagine the boundaries of Asia as defined by legacies of European colonialism and Cold War politics, and the Middle East is often left out of "Asia."

Emi Grate, a Brooklyn-based Burmese drag queen, curates a pan-Asian drag show called *A+*; she imagines Asia and its diasporas expansively (hence the plus sign). I was so glad to see the inclusion of Louisiana-based Lemon Pop, a Palestinian American queen, in a 2020 summer lineup of *A+*. Lemon Pop, in a variety of feminine guises, lip-synched to "Ramadan El Sana Di," a Muslim kids' song in English, French, and Arabic celebrating Ramadan.

The inclusion of Lemon Pop in this line-up of Asian acts refuses the arbitrary boundaries of the Asian continent's geography that divide up the Middle East/ Southwest Asia from the rest of the land. Furthermore, including a Palestinian Muslim artist in the lineup is a gesture of solidarity with Palestine's ongoing resistance to settler colonialism. Lemon Pop's choice of song, while easily dismissed as multicultural flippancy in its childishness, reveals the multilingual and therefore colonial legacies of the Arab world. Performing a song about Ramadan makes apparent her Muslim-ness, and

refuses xenophobic generalizations that suggest there is
no room for queerness/drag in Islam, doing so without
pandering to orientalist visions of the exotic.

Emi Grate's curation redraws the imagined borders
of Asia, borders defined by centuries of colonization
from within and outside of the continent, as well as by
post-Cold War imaginations of geopolitical divides. In
turn, Lemon Pop's performance elides an Orientalist
gesture, by resisting a performance of the exotic East.
By playing with gender, these performers reimagine
geography.

Carcerality / Criminality

Confinement has been central to securing colonial
power, and particularly for disciplining minoritarian
people into state-sanctioned gender formations.[151] Such
carceral forms include the US prison-industrial complex that disproportionately criminalizes Black, Latinx,
and Indigenous people, as well as Residential Schools
for Native Americans and First Nations people in North
America, Magdalene Asylums for sex workers in Ireland,
and Uyghur "re-education camps" in China.

One way of executing colonial power through
carcerality is by criminalizing certain groups of people. In Chapter 1, I described the Criminal Tribes Act

of 1871 in India, and how this now-defunct policy labels particular caste, Indigenous, and gender groups as prone to criminality, and has been used as a model for more contemporary legislation. One example is the Karnataka Police Act 36A that, since 2011, required hijras to register with local authorities and to request permission to move between neighborhoods; these restrictions provide a cover for police to abuse their power through arrest, blackmail, and sexual violence.[152]

At the 2012 Bangalore Pride march, two trans activists, Gee and Bittu, dressed as policemen to protest KPA 36A. They paired the unmistakable khaki-green jackets and peaked caps of India's police with fun, bright-colored shorts, and painted on vivid blue, green, and orange facial hair in the large curly shapes often sported by South Indian policemen. Their cheerful fashions fit in with the sequins, rainbows, and glitter littering the visual landscape of the march, but the uniforms also made these two drag kings stand out from the crowd. There was, as always, a substantial police presence at the periphery of the march, ensuring we kept our walk within the streets space designated. Gee and Bittu's styling was contrasting enough to not be mistaken as police, or to be threatening to the cops—some even took pictures with the two drag kings who goofily shook fake clubs and made overexaggerated stern looks.

However, as they danced, marched, held up plac-
ards, and chanted, they called for the repeal of KPA 36A.
They used police drag to decry the transphobic carceral
logics of this legislation, while also laughing at the phal-
lic masculinity of the police. I don't mean to deny the
real violence that police inflict. However, drag provided
an opportunity to laugh at police rather than remain
compliant subjects as they regulated our queer and trans
bodies at the march. It's difficult work to make drag that
speaks directly to political urgencies but still revels in
the chaotic, colorful, joyful spectacles of queer style.
Gee and Bittu's rainbow police characters at Bangalore
Pride are one example—they danced to the Dalit drum-
mers' beats, and sung chants, while also making a state-
ment about police collusion with transphobic violence.

Japanese-American Politi-Kween, Kristi Yummykochi, developed "Never Again is Now" as a response
to the incarceration of young people who were forcibly separated from their families upon arriving at the
US-Mexico border during the Trump administra-
tion. Kristi, based in San Francisco, is part of the Asian
American drag ensemble the Rice Rockettes. When
her performance began at their summer 2019 show,
I braced for a somber tone as the projected background
video started to play: "February 19th, 1942" followed

by archival photographs of internment campgrounds and anti-Japanese posters and graffiti. In response to the bombing of Pearl Harbor, Franklin Roosevelt had ordered the relocation of Japanese Americans into internment camps under Executive Order 9066. Kristi's family was incarcerated during World War II, and her uncle was born in a concentration camp in Arkansas.

Against the backdrop of an internment camp photograph, Kristi enters in a floral kimono, lip-synching Nao's "In the Morning." Two men enter, with ICE (Immigration and Customs Enforcement) logos on their all-black clothing, removing her kimono to reveal a US-flag dress underneath. With scissors, they cut the dress off her body, and leave her "naked" in her drag undergarments standing in front of a tarpaulin-covered box. Kristi removes the cover to reveal that the box is a cage. When she crawls inside, she immediately conjures images of the caged Central American children so familiar from news coverage of detention facilities along the US-Mexico border. The image is immediately heartbreaking.

The internment camp photo fades, and cherry blossom-like feathers flutter down on the screen; the song shifts to Beyoncé's "Love Drought." Other drag queens, Kristi's Rice Rockette sisters, escort her out of the cage and dress her in a frilly, sequined rainbow coat. She decorates the stage in garlands of origami cranes as bubbles flutter through the air around a banner that reads "Abolish ICE."

Kristi layers two different scenes of imprisonment, 1940s Japanese internment and ongoing border detentions of undocumented migrants, making clear the racialized nature of incarceration. While Kristi asked us to read her as Japanese American, with her Kimono layered over a US flag and internment camp image in the background, it was ICE agents who stripped her of her "citizenship." ICE only came into formation in 2003 in the wake of post-9/11 militarization and securitization of US borders. This anachronistic use of ICE is an important detail that layers the histories of incarceration on each other. Similarly, the laying of origami crane garlands over the "Abolish Ice" banner and on top of the cage recalls the annual ritual of memorializing Japanese interment. Though she doesn't make her family's intimate history apparent in the performance, her body stands in for her family's and other Japanese Americans. At the same time, her performance also calls for justice for ongoing imprisonments.

Kristi is certainly not the only drag performer to make work about Japanese internment. Japanese-Irish

drag artist and founder of UK-based Asian queer
performance collective The Bitten Peach, ShayShay,
performs in the kimonos their grandmother managed to
hold on to through her time in the internment camps.[153]
Performance artist TT Takemoto, in their video *Looking
for Jiro Onuma*, takes on a drag king aesthetic. They perform "homoerotic breadmaking" and lipsynch to ABBA
as Onuma, an interned mess hall worker, reimagines
the feminized labor expected of interned Asian men as
pleasurable and queer.[154] Like Takemoto, Kristi brings
a sense of play and beauty to remembering internment,
but she goes further to think about Japanese internment
alongside ongoing border detentions. Placing the origami garlands over the cage and banner, dancing and
lip-synching sweetly in her glittering robe, she conjures
a future in which multiple violations of human dignity
are being memorialized, over but never forgotten.

Enslavement

Colonialism has not only turned land into property, but
people too. The transatlantic slave trade that forcibly
relocated Africans into the Americas and elsewhere was,
as described in Chapter 1, predicated on the queer genders that Europeans assigned to Black bodies. As such,
drag is an opportunity to indulge in the mess of gender,

as a way of laughing at colonial formations and practicing freedom in the club.

Like Chanel Mercedez-Benz, Miss Toto too renders a scene of fugitivity, specifically Harriet Tubman's escape from enslavement and her abolitionist work in the Underground Railroad. Nineteenth-century maverick Tubman was born into slavery in Maryland in 1822, and following her escape in 1849, she helped scores of other enslaved people out of captivity by escorting them along the Underground Railroad, a trail of secret safe houses and hideouts that led to northern territories—a complicated story to tell in a five-minute drag number.

At a *Double Stubble* party in Miami, Florida, a feminine voice, probably ripped from a YouTube documentary, comes through the speakers: "Harriet Tubman began her life in the bonds of slavery, but lived her life helping others achieve their freedom." Miss Toto, a Black, muscular drag queen, walks on stage shuffling a broom over the floor to the opening beats of Britney Spears's "I'm a Slave 4 U." She sacrifices the glamor of club drag for a plain white dress, and a white headscarf over her curly black wig; she's also barefoot, a rare sight in the club, and especially on the drag stage where high heels are so central to signaling femininity.

As she dances to Spears's song, swirling the folds of her skirt, pumping her hips and chest, Miss Toto depicts Tubman as an unruly and agential figure, even as she declares, "I'm a, slaaaaave, for you!" Her use of this song lays bare the unmarked nature of whiteness, such that Spears can call herself a slave without recalling histories of violence. A white pop star's empowered sexuality as a slave suddenly conjures messy feelings when put on the Black body—could slaves, as property, have agency over their sexuality? Drag can disrupt nightlife's good and sexy feelings to raise difficult questions. But also please don't cancel Britney; things are much more complicated when we consider the revelation that Britney's labor and mobility were tightly controlled by her family well into adulthood.

The song unexpectedly shifts to nineties throwback "C'mon N' Ride It (The Train)" by Quad City DJ's. The audience realizes quickly that "train" becomes a metonym for "railroad," and Miss Toto picks up a small lantern, an iconographic object associated with both the Underground Railroad and portraits of Harriet Tubman. Lantern in hand, Miss Toto jumps off the stage, pressing through the crowd. She scours to find two Black people. They are surprised and giggling as she holds their hands and escorts them through the thicket of bodies to a front-row spot. She looks around again, finds another Black person, and ushers them over the stage, to the place where she has safely brought the other fugitives. Her performance ends with a lip-synch to Carly Rae Jepsen's "Run Away With Me," a fun white-girl anthem that Miss Toto as Harriet Tubman repurposes to call other Black people to escape the bonds and logics of slavery.

By physically bringing Black folks together in the club and escorting them to the front of the show, Miss Toto privileges Black community in nightlife spaces that can often be anti-Black and alienating. Through hilarious audience interaction, she uses the ruse of Harriet Tubman to reconfigure who is given importance in predominantly white spaces. Miss Toto's performance ends with her pulling off the headscarf which lifts into the air a cloud of glitter and the audience goes wild, a cathartic ending to this heroic tale.

Brooklyn-based Black queen Merrie Cherry offers a performance that is as climactic, but without that final release that Miss Toto's affords, at least not for the audience. Merrie, with a simple short dress and a blindfold over her eyes sits on a stool facing the audience; she lip-synchs to Nina Simone's "Four Women" (if you don't know the song, I recommend giving it a quick listen!). In the song, Simone sings in the character of four different Black women, of different skin colors and hair types, with different names: Aunt Sarah, Saffronia, Sweet Thing, and Peaches. Simone's characters each narrate their stories in the first person, calling attention to the manual and sexual servitude of slavery. These women are not blind to the conditions of their lives, so why does Merrie wear a blindfold? I've seen Merrie do this number two times, and there's also a recording of one more on YouTube; to me the blindfold withholds *our* access to her, prevents us from looking into her eyes to know she is Merrie Cherry and *not* these women.

Sitting in the chair, Merrie Cherry lip-synchs to the words of Simone; when the characters switch, she removes the wig on her head and a stagehand assists her in putting on another, one that matches the description sung by the woman.[155] Watching Merrie's performances of "Four Women" it is so evident to me that she is fully committed to the song, but the blindfold tells me she is not there to engage us or to entertain us. Without the comfort of her looking back at me, I have to look at her Black feminine body in light of the song she sings, and understand that her very body is evidence of the survival work of Black women that Peaches sings about, screams about, in the final verse of Simone's song. This song about Black history, bodies, and gender is embodied in

Merrie herself, as she makes herself "fungible," malleable to the figures in the song, susceptible to the looks that we place on her.

By denying us the returned gaze she limits reciprocity with the audience, she does not give us closure! Leaving the story unfinished, she places the burden on the audience to imagine their relation to and culpability with her oppression.

Protest

Colonial violence has always engendered resistance, and I want to close this chapter by centering drag's explicit response to colonial instruments.

In the first months of the COVID-19 pandemic, both protest and drag had to find ways to thrive online, especially in the US, where the state's response to the pandemic was paltry, to say the least. The emergencies produced by the pandemic exacerbated systemic inequalities, including access to medical care and private space/shelter. The spread of the novel coronavirus, understood to originate in China, reignited anti-Asian sentiments across the globe. These xenophobic attacks included verbal abuse and physical attacks on phenotypically Asian folks, regardless of whether they were Chinese. Vancouver-based Asian Canadian drag artist Shay Dior created a digital drag video in the Summer of 2020 titled "Contaminated by Racism," that she describes as "a call to action to end the rise in COVID-19 fueled racism and xenophobia against the Asian community around the world."

As the instrumental opening of Banks's "Contaminated" hums in, we see Shay staring into a mirror, a black mask over the lower half of her face. She removes it to reveal a biohazard symbol drawn around her mouth; the black curves of the symbol look claw-like on her skin. In queer communities, biohazard symbols are familiar; HIV positive people sometimes get the symbol tattooed on their bodies, a strategy for destigmatizing living with the virus by uncloseting their status. Performing for a primarily queer audience, Shay's use of the symbol in her makeup signals multiple histories of pathologization: early twentieth-century associations of the Asian migrant with disease;[156] HIV stigma; and Coronavirus transmission. Shay's drag mixes masculine and feminine aesthetics. She feminizes her face with a heavy contour and thick black eyeliner, but she also has short, buzzed hair, a chinstrap for facial hair, a mesh shirt, and leather collar. Her lip-synch is mournful; she assumes a fetal position and raps desperately against the wall on which are projected news clippings about anti-Asian violence.

Toward the end of the video, she puts a surgical mask over her mouth which reads: "End your racism." Another one over it: "I am an artist." Another: "I am a frontline worker." And finally: "I am not a virus." Shay lets her body speak in multitudes, allowing her femininity and masculinity to coexist, but also mapping her body as a biohazard through makeup while writing on a mask "I am not a virus." In doing so, she calls attention both to the ways her body is seen and makes explicit the way she wants us to see her. Removing mask, after mask, after mask, she plays with "the reveal," a central gesture in burlesque and drag to surprise the audience by discarding a piece of clothing. But instead of revealing the biohazard makeup as she did in the first shot, she rechoreographs the reveal to layer urgent political messages on each other.

I conclude with Shay not only because her performance feels so urgent in its uptake of themes related to COVID and Anti-Asian violence, but because she exemplifies the quick ways that drag adapts its aesthetics and medium to sociopolitical contexts. This is one of the things I love about drag as an artform, its capacity to swiftly adjust and recalibrate to colonialism's perpetually shifting and multi-scaled entrapments.

Racialized bodies are constantly being managed through pathologization, incarceration, exoticization, labor extraction, and land dispossession. Drag can mobilize the aesthetics of gender, race, Indigeneity, class, and disability to recall and speak back to multiple and overlapping legacies of colonialism. The performances I've described do all this with humor, elegance, urgency, and wit. This combination of play and urgency suggest there is an alternative condition to the histories of violence they invoke; other worlds are possible. In this chapter I have focused on select performances, but each of these acts exacts its excellence through a variety of small choices: music, dress, makeup, choreography, location, etc. In the next chapter, I offer a toolkit for doing drag in ways that attend to these minor choices, choices that play a significant role in the capacity for performance to make other worlds possible.

Chapter 5

JUST DO IT!
TECHNIQUES AND TECHNOLOGIES
FOR DECOLONIZING DRAG

Alisha Boti Kabab, one of LaWhore Vagistan's drag daughters, performed at a *Jai Ho!* party in Chicago dressed in a women's "Punjabi suit," a long, billowing top and comfortable printed loose pants that matched her dupatta (scarf), which was pinned into her hair. As usual, she wore no makeup and had a beard. "I love this outfit, it looks so good on you," I said. "Thank you! I stole it, um, I 'borrowed' it from my mum's closet."

Alisha lived with her parents then, and they didn't approve of her queerness, nor her drag. When she was at these queer Bollywood parties, she would tell her parents she was at a medical school study group, or at the library preparing for a major exam. In drag, she doesn't wear makeup in order to avoid returning home with traces of glitter and paint on her body; but then again, her performance never actually needs it! Once on stage Alisha wowed us with her controlled claps and careful kicks, the signature moves of *giddha*, a Punjabi women's dance. In her dress and dance, she conjured the Punjabi aunty so authentically it didn't matter that she didn't have any makeup on.

Alisha's drag, which relies on makeshift outfits, keeps a beard, and avoids makeup, returns us to this book's beginning; she was one of the performers that night who were dismissed as "not real drag queens." She reminds me that we need to expand what we call drag in order to redistribute the cultural and material capital that this art form has accrued. Her drag reflects the assertion that gender is made through the assemblage of meanings on the body, not just one identifier, that tips the scales of masculinity and femininity, or perhaps allows them to exist in abundance on the same body, or maybe allows gender to become something else altogether. But Alisha's circumstances reveal that people do drag within limits, within the financial constraints of student life, and the moral constraints of diasporic respectability politics.

Alisha's fugitive acts—nicking her mom's clothing and lying about her whereabouts—ask us to offer her grace as she does drag in ways that don't reflect the polished aesthetics that the scene so highly praises. Then again, her dance moves are *so* fierce, *so* spot on, *so* transformative, perhaps she doesn't even need makeup or expensive costumes.

I use "technology" to refer to the *things* we put on and take off the body to make gendered meaning—hair, nails, clothing, shoes, accessories, prosthetic body parts etc. I use "technique" to refer to the way we *use* the body to create meaning—crossing legs, squaring shoulders, swaying hips, flexing feet, clenching jaws, etc. Techniques and technologies are complementary. Alisha's *technique*, her movements and gestures, make and remake gender in ways that amplify some of the *technology* she's employed, her mother's outfit, and mute others like her facial and body hair. Here I'm calling back to Eve Sedgwick's threshold effect of gender from Chapter 1.

People often ask me if I "become a different person" when I do drag, and I like to say, "LaWhore is just Kareem after two vodka-sodas." Truth be told, I don't do a lot of character work to develop LaWhore's spoken or body language, the vodka-sodas just help numb the pain of wearing six-inch heels for hours. But these technologies do in fact transform my technique: my body feels the difference and performs accordingly.

Balancing in heels, bound in corset, wide in my hip-pads, and boobs (a pair of socks) pressing on my chest, my weight shifts forward and my arms sit differently by my side; I feel more comfortable with the feminine hand-on-hip placement, and my lazy posture is lifted upward. With long fingernails glued on, I'm less likely to ball up my fist in that masculine way; rather, I gesture widely with fingers splayed. Lengthened eye-lashes, billowing fabrics, the smell of glue, sequin tex-tures, the hard knock of high heels, heavy jewelry on my earlobes, wrists, and fingers, long hair hitting the middle of my back, all of these make me *feel* different, and they choreograph my body in un-usual ways; they change my technique. I then choreograph my move-ments to gesture to these new additions to my body, fluttering my fingers over my face to draw attention to my lengthened eyelashes and meticulous makeup.

Technologies and techniques are complementary; they amplify, neutralize, and contradict each other. Pouting my lips will have different effects on an audience member if I have on a mustache instead of over-drawn lips, and a different effect all together if I have both! I understand also that technologies and the fleshy body also overlap: hair, muscles, and wide hips may already be part of the body. For those who do have them, we can disguise these features, *or* accentuate them depending on the illusion we want to create.

While I shave my facial hair and layer two different foundations to mask the beard shadow, bearded perform-ers will actually darken or glitter their beards to make them pop on stage. Also, while I wear pads that give me the illusion of rounder hips and bum, more buxom queens use corsets to accentuate their own breasts and hips. To create a gendered attribute that we might not already have, we can use various kinds of prosthetics to give the illusion that we do. Hence, I don't necessarily differentiate these fleshy parts of the body from what I'm describing as technologies.

In this chapter, I turn to a few techniques and technologies of drag to think about their collusion in and resistance to colonial and racist logics. Below are a series of hot takes on some of the common ways that we do drag. For those of us already in the drag scene, this is an opportunity to pause and consider how we're participating in colonized ideologies of the body, gender, race, and nation. For those who've never done drag, I hope you'll see this as a starter kit, a smorgasbord to pick and choose from—amateur drag avenues are as productive worlds of critical intervention as the mainstage of *RuPaul's Drag Race*.[157]

I will go in a kind of "order," starting with choosing a drag name, to imagining costume choices, and eventually anticipating the location of your shows. Ultimately, I'm not suggesting that any of these is the right or wrong thing to do. As I've laid out in the first half of the book, while the globalized gender binary is a colonial infliction, for Black and Brown subjects, the stakes of conforming to or deviating from gender norms vary from context to context. Depending on the situation, interrupting the status quo and reproducing it both have their place in rendering a decolonial critique, and crafting pleasure in the face of discipline.

By breaking things down into the bits and pieces of drag, I hope drag becomes *more* available to those who want to try it, and gives those who witness it more tools to carefully interpret and enjoy it.

Call me by your drag name

In my early research on South Asian LGBTQ nightlife, I found it hard to locate and interview *desi* drag artists. This is not to say that drag wasn't happening in South Asian spaces, but that it just wasn't happening regularly in nightclubs. More often, it showed up as casual performances at house parties. One of the reasons I couldn't find any one particular king or queen was because in these less formalized spaces, performers would assume a different name each time they performed, often the name of the Bollywood star they were mimicking for the night: Rekha, Parveen, Meena.

But when you need to be recognizable in clubs and pageants and on TV and social media, having a signature name becomes necessary. Your drag name is often the first thing people know about you. It is a way of signaling your personality, politics, geographic origins, and gender.

Taking on a drag name and building a persona and history around that name is a valuable technique to show off one's political placement. It's not uncommon for queens to gesture to their hometowns and countries of origin in their drag names. My own drag name, LaWhore Vagistan, envisions alternative geopolitics based on my family's history. I am Sindhi, meaning I am part of the ethnolinguistic community from Sindh, a territory in Pakistan. However, during the 1947 partition of Pakistan and India, my Hindu grandparents were displaced into India because of the arbitrary border drawn by the British colonial government to differentiate the new Hindu and Muslim nations. We became Indian by default, and the ever-burgeoning nationalisms that differentiate India and Pakistan suggest that I should pledge allegiance to India, even though I was born in Gibraltar and raised in Ghana (both British colonial territories, Gibraltar remains annexed by the UK). And so, my first name refers to Lahore in Pakistan to refuse the disavowal of India I'm expected to perform as a Sindhi Hindu. Visualized by imprinting an anatomical drawing over the subcontinent, Vagistan insists on the sexualized nature of the subcontinent and rescripts it as a more capacious body or system that stretches into Iran and China. The name, for me, acknowledges that sexuality and sexual violence were always central to the project of colonial fracture and nation making.

Intersex Black drag queen and performance artist Vaginal Crème Davis comes to her name as a tribute to Angela Davis, the scholar, activist, and member of the Black Panther Party. Her decision to riff on Angela Davis's name was a means of identifying with a Black radical tradition while also avoiding the hetero-masculinity of the Black Panthers. This is what scholar José Esteban Muñoz has famously described as "disidentification," working within and around the limits of expected identity performance to instead foreground critique, pleasure, and survival.[158] Amongst the Sisters of Perpetual Indulgence, a global sorority of drag artist-activists who raise money for HIV/AIDS research and education, Los Angeles-based Sister Mary-Kohn stands out as another excellent disidentifier. A Chicana drag nun, she uses the form of nun's nomenclature to play with the Spanish epithet *maricon* used against gay men, calling attention simultaneously to the homophobia of both Mexican machismo and Catholicism.[159] Spelling the name as Kohn also recalls the dastardly closeted gay lawyer Roy Cohn, immortalized in Tony Kushner's play *Angels in America*. Referencing Cohn points to the institutional hypocrisies and failures in the response to the HIV/AIDS crisis that render the The Sisters' fundraising efforts so urgent.

Some artists use their drag names as a way of opening up the meanings placed on them and complicating the genders they are supposed to perform. For example, Johnny T keeps the simple last name to signify multiple meanings: "testosterone, tranny, trouble, T-birds, Travolta."[160] Brooklyn-Based Asian American artist Untitled Queen's name refuses the kind of cutesy racialized wordplay that some Asian drag queens draw on to make themselves legible: Manila Luzon, Kim Chi, BaeJing, Jasmine Rice, LaWhore Vagistan, Masala Sapphire, etc. This is not to say that these names are not valuable in the bold ways they insist upon their Asian-ness. However, Untitled Queen offers a necessary alternative to the pressures of conforming to racialized expectations as well.

Naming oneself, avoiding legible names, or constantly switching names are all strategies for (dis)locating drag in the gendered geographies of (post)colonial maps.

Face! Face! Face!

Drag artists rely on makeup to highlight and redraw facial features in ways that conform to and contort masculine or feminine ideals. A bright foundation is used to lighten areas that we want to appear raised on the face, and darker tones create the illusion of shadows that make other parts of the face look inset. By creating new light and dark areas on the face, we reorganize the face shape. While offering a virtual makeup tutorial, the poet Wo Chan, who performs as drag queen The Illustrious Pearl, told the audience that they don't narrow Pearl's nose when they contour. Pearl explained that contouring the nose, drawing a thinner bright line down the long ridge and darkening the sides around it, is meant to create a more beautiful narrow nose. This ideal nose shape is a distinctly white one, and Pearl explained how ethnic groups who sometimes have flatter noses, Black, Indigenous, and Asian folks in particular, are bullied and ridiculed for their natural nose shape.

It's up to you how you want to shape your nose, what you think suits your face and style. Maybe makeup is an opportunity to have a different nose than the one you've been bullied for and to enjoy the kindness and attention and tips that come with that. Or maybe you're putting on white glamor in order to critique it. All this is to say, even the simplest task of shaping the nose or lips or eyes is predicated on racialized aesthetics and the ubiquity of white supremacy in mundane life.

When I first started doing drag, I didn't have much of a clue as to what I was supposed to be doing with makeup. I blended my contour shadows in the wrong direction, if I even blended at all. I didn't intuitively understand the play of light and shape that makeup was supposed to accomplish. At a nightclub competition called "Drag Class" in Austin, TX, LaWhore was adopted by a mentor, a stunning white spooky queen named Rhonda Jewels, who finally taught her the way around a makeup brush. And yet, the competition judges kept critiquing us for LaWhore's non-apparent lip and poor highlight. Eventually, a Black drag queen who was guest-judging one night clocked the problem: "She doesn't have the right makeup for her darker skin color." Makeup is often designed with a lighter skin in mind, and it interacts with light differently based on the skin it's sitting on. While brands like Fenty and Juvia's Place designed for more melanated complexions are now popular, it took some wrangling then to find the right powders and bases for all my makeup to fully show up on that stage.

Figuring out what color to be in drag is its own reckoning. Because you want all your artistry and newly drawn-on features to be legible in the dim light of the club, the tendency, particularly for artists of color, is to apply a foundation that is generally lighter than one's skin tone. Just because dark-skinned queens use a lighter foundation for the stage does not necessarily mean that they are caught up in assimilationist aesthetics. Rather, it is technologies of makeup and lighting that have not been calibrated for dark skin.

More generally, using colors not natural to human skin becomes a way of escaping the traps of racial representation. For example, Toronto-based Mango Sassi presents her South Asian-ness through her name, riffing on the sweet milky fruity drink, mango lassi. Mango covers her face, neck, and upper chest in purple, blue, green, or yellow foundations, and contours with lighter and darker shades of those colors. She then matches her leggings and gloves so that her entire body appears to be that color. In doing so, she opts out of the racial regimes of the cosmetic industry and its range of "nude" colors that always skew toward light skin. She also skirts the expectation to perform exotic South Asian-ness for the consumable pleasure of predominantly white audiences.

There are of course white drag queens who paint in full color as well, and this can function as a strategy to obscure their whiteness. There are also several instances of white queens in blackface,[161] and Latina queens darkening their makeup when lip-synching the songs of Black divas.[162] Blackface, like yellow, red, and brown face, has been used by white theatre practitioners over the last few centuries to mimic and mock subordinated racial others, Black, East Asian, Native American, and Arab/South Asian people respectively.

For Australia-based Aboriginal drag artist Andrew Farrell, a member of the Wodi Wodi clan, their light skin becomes the grounds for strangers to challenge their claims to Indigenous heritage. To reflect this white fragility back to others, Farrell paints their face "clown white" and adopts the name "Becky."[163] Here, drag name and makeup, technique and technology, work in tandem to reflect whiteness back to white people.

None of these technologies singularly excise us from the aesthetic regimes of whiteness—whiteness has sutured itself into so many modes of representation—but they offer opportunities to negotiate racial difference on stage on our own terms once we've taken the time to learn their history and study their effects.

(Un)Dressing Up

In 2016, LaWhore Vagistan released a music video for a song called "Sari," a parody of Justin Bieber's hit song "Sorry." She sings:

> I don't want to look like all of the other drag queens.
> Leggings for days, dresses for miles, and gowns for weeks.
> Chanel and Dior, Louis Vuitton, Versace.
> 'Cuz I look best, when I'm dressed, like an Aunty.

Measuring her fashion against branded, tight-fitting, glamorous mainstream drag, she instead celebrates the figure of the aunty, associated more with home than the club. Clothing is so central to drag *and* to gender. But there are indeed dominant aesthetics in drag scenes that privilege the tight-fitted cocktail dress or gown that exhibits the feminine silhouette a queen has created will be seen, or the broad-shouldered suit jacket for drag kings that conveniently hides breasts.

Though I've been trying to stage permutations of drag across the globe, there are instances where conservative parties in non-Western nations will ignore local histories of gender variance, and claim that drag and/or queerness are white, colonial infiltrations. It's a convenient tactic that misuses the logic of decolonization to enforce heteropatriarchy. In these cases, dress becomes a very valuable tool for drag because it so efficiently signals national and ethnic belonging.[164] At Pride festivals in Johannesburg, the many kinds of dress that drag artists wear localize their queerness as distinctly African: "One marcher wore a Xhosa outfit in orange cotton with black braid trim and accompanying head wrap. Another displayed the distinctive headpiece worn by Zulu women. Yet two more donned the Herero 'long dress.'"[165] For Kanaka Maoli drag queen Cocoa Chandelier, using kahili feathers recalls her Indigenous ancestry, even while her Victorian-style dress evidences the legacy of colonialism.[166] Cocoa's holikii dress "is reminiscent of the dresses worn by women of the Ka'ahumanu Society—a mostly Christian Congregationalist Hawaiian organization known through the islands."[167] Queen Ka'ahumanu was an early convert to Christianity upon British settlement in the early nineteenth century. By combining dress and feathers, Cocoa uses costume to both reflect Indigeneity back to her Kanaka Maoli audience, while also invoking histories of colonization and religious conversion.

If costume is meant to transform one's body or gender in drag, what happens when it in fact reveals the body beneath it in unexpected ways? At the prime of her career, Tejana singer Rita Vidaurri was one of few

women to perform in Mexico wearing *charro* pants, the
fitted, embroidered trouser associated with Mariachi
singers, styled on the garments of Mexican horsemen.
This kind of dress, associated with masculine nation-
alism, rusticity, and militarism not only signifies something different on a woman's body, but it fit Vidaurri's
curvy body differently.[168] When we look closely at
Vidaurri's style, rather than seeing the female body and
masculine clothing in contradiction, our imaginations
are stretched to see different kinds of gender and desire
come into being when such costume switches happen.
Think back to my discussion of bearded drag, when
I talked about the abundance of gender signifiers on the
body requiring creativity both on the part of the performer *and* the audience. A student once said to me after
watching LaWhore dance to a popular Bollywood song
in a sari: "I know these songs, I know this form of dress,
I know these moves, but *I didn't know how to watch them
on your body.*" She was referring to my hairy, bearded,
soft-voiced, soft-textured body that she expected to
perform as a "professor," elbow-patched jacket and all,
instead of rolling on the classroom floor in six yards of
pink and gold fabric.

Our ways of seeing gender are stretched in exciting ways in these moments. A different kind of

erotics is possible between audience and performer when Vidaurri's feminine embodiment stretches the *charro* pant physically and metaphorically.[169] We learn to know, enjoy, and desire gender in more expansive ways.

There are so many forms of dress that bind gender and nation/ethnicity/race: the Filipino terno, the Japanese kimono, the Chinese qipao, the Mexican zoot suit.[170] Mobilizing these forms of dress in drag performance, putting them on unexpected bodies or moving in them in non-traditional ways, is a valuable way of interrogating nationalist histories *and* discursive constructions of racial difference. Refusing these garments altogether is another valuable choice too, especially for Indigenous, tribal, and minoritarian people who have been marginalized or brutalized by nationalist agendas, and who might find putting on these garments, even to reinvent them, too constricting. Sometimes, the suits, gowns, or other dress of global whiteness can offer sanctuary from national costumes that have a more locally charged meaning.

Taking off clothing in drag performance is its own engagement with race and gender. It is not uncommon to see drag artists dispel the "illusion" they're performing by removing clothing that is meant to reinvent their gender—snatching their wig off or fully disrobing.

This can appear as both an act of soft vulnerability or a highly sensational moment of nakedness. These gestures sometimes suggest there is indeed an "authentic" gender beneath the drag, as *RuPaul's Drag Race* contestant Milan does when lip-synching to Lady Gaga's "Born This Way." For artists of color, this dramatic gesture can also reveal the dark skin and tightly curled black hair or bald head[171] that has been covered up by accoutrements of white femininity such as long blonde hair and sequined gowns.[172] For Kristi Yummykochi's performance, discussed in Chapter 4, changing costume or removing clothing mid-performance was an important means of critical storytelling in drag, staging race, nationality, and vulnerability.

At a 2018 drag show in San Juan Puerto Rico, Pó Rodil began their performance as a debonair king with a little salsa in his step, and then stripped out of the formal masculine garments to reveal a fleshy belly with "O'NEILL VIOLADOR" painted on it. Their friend climbed on stage to stand with Rodil, and suddenly the image of them together became all too familiar to the audience present. A year prior, Rodil and this same friend were photographed at the May Day protests, where activists decried austerity measures—particularly the cessation of many social services—that the island faced due to the local government's negligence.

Puerto Rico, as an unincorporated territory of the United States, is one of the oldest colonies in the world; its financial crisis is due in part to the limited federal funding the US offers the territory in comparison to mainland states. To blame for the ongoing crisis is both a highly distrusted local government and irresponsible US oversight. At the protest, Rodil painted on their bare torso "O'NEILL VIOLADOR" referring to politician Héctor O'Neill who was accused (but not charged) of sexual assault. Naming O'Neill's sexual violence proved controversial, and some activists pushed against Rodil and friends' action, suggesting that *this* protest was not about sexuality or gender issues. A photograph of Rodil with their friend then went viral, and was memed to mock their radical politics, fat brown body, and gender non-conformity.

Relying on the contrast as they undress, from the legibly masculine salsero to the gender-ambiguous activist, Rodil uses clothing *and* its removal to reinscribe their political protest, as well as to assert the fabulous and sexy gender ambiguity of their fat, trans body that has been derided by Right and Left media alike.[173]

These manipulations of clothing are not new. The famed Jewel Box Revue, touring in the fifties and sixties, teased the audience that there was one woman in the cast of "female impersonators." That woman was not hiding amongst the drag queens, she was in fact famed Black performer and activist Stormé DeLarverie performing as the masculine emcee. Rather than revealing a feminine persona masqueraded by a deft execution of masculinity, Stormé used the reveal to show off her butch queer masculinity.[174] While the "reveal" has returned as a staple gesture in drag shows—thanks Roxxxy Andrews, Violet Chachki, and Sasha Velour!— taking off, putting on, and repurposing garments during a performance are *all* ways of exercising critique in drag.

Location! Location! Location!

Choosing *where* you do drag—on the street, in the club, at home, in the library—is also an opportunity to think about the relationships of power, history and the body, and to consider how we keep both entertainers and audiences safe. Early scholarly research on drag from the 1970s details the differences between show queens, who have access to expensive costumes and are regularly invited to perform on stage and headline shows, and street queens, who occupy public spaces such as streets and parks in order to sell sex.[175] While street queens could sometimes get club gigs, they supplemented their income with sex work, which made them more vulnerable to violence and harassment. There is still some continuity between drag and sex work scenes; I risk saying this knowing that US right-wing lobbyists would like you to believe that all drag is meant to be sexual, and therefore supposedly dangerous to children, but this claim is simply not true! There is also continuity between theatrical drag performance and everyday embodiments of transness as discussed in Chapter 1. Here is another moment to expand what kind of drag we legitimate, to invite those who don't have the expensive resources of elite glamor to the drag stage, in order to redistribute income, and provide a safer/more private space to perform, as well as to do sex work.

The setting and backdrop you perform against can indeed amplify aspects of gender, race, and class. Watching the red velvet curtains part to reveal the queens at Parliament House in Orlando made the show feel expensive and fabulous. Meanwhile, watching performers on the one-foot-high carpeted stage of Town Hall Pub in Chicago made the performance feel makeshift regardless of how impressive the entertainer was. The home can be an important place for drag, it can be safer than the nightclub, and the mutual under-standing between guests at a house party can bring a level of respect and care to witnessing others perform. The working assumption in gay clubs is that the gender beneath the drag performer's costume is different from the one they are performing, that the drag queen is really a gay man and the drag king is in fact a lesbian. This might dissuade trans men and women from performing in a nightclub or for strangers.

In my ethnographic research on queer South Asian nightlife in India and the US, I've witnessed drag shows in backyards, rooftops, living rooms, churches, NGO offices, and community centers. None of these spaces offered the intensity of the nightclub with its state-of-the-art speaker systems, raised stage, and mesmerizing lighting. However, they did provide a level of warmth and privacy for minoritarian subjects, many of whom were not out beyond the group that had gathered.

Documenting a daytime drag performance by two Afro-Cuban drag kings in their humble home on the peripheries of Havana, ethnomusicologist M. Leslie Santana observed the many possibilities of drag at home.[176] Props and costume changes were quickly available, music could be chosen in an instant based on mood and requests, food was served, and the performers could capitalize on their familiarity with the audience to make jokes and interact. For these working-class Cuban kings, being able to host a daytime show in their home gave them a control of the event in ways that clubs, which usually privilege queens and cosmopolitan glamor, rarely afford.

While many of the examples I offer across this book are situated in the nightclub, here the living room in suburban Havana is repurposed into a drag salon. In rural Kentucky, queer youth have turned the aisles of Walmart into a fashion catwalk.[177] Drag belongs wherever you want it to, it just takes a little tipping of the scales to turn the sterile corporate megastore into a scene of fabulosity, to turn the quaint living room into a quirky cabaret.

Tipping the scales

Pakistani-Lebanese drag artist Faluda Islam, performing at the Queens Museum in 2017, distributed small envelopes filled with paper currency from a variety of countries to their audience. Tipping often works as praise for cultural artists like hijras, erotic dancers, tour guides, masseuses, and buskers. US drag artists rely on tips to supplement their paltry compensation, but tipping is also its own gesture of intimacy and affirmation as audience and performer come into proximity.[178] It's a consensual moment of transaction and touch between strangers. Have you ever tipped a drag performer, and they held on to your hand and looked into your eyes a little bit longer than it takes to accept the bill, making you feel like a star, feel rich, feel important? When a drag king invites you to slip your tip into his dildo-stuffed jockstrap, he invites you to see him as sexy, as a desirable subject right there in front of you, rather than pretend he is a distant asexual entertainer. In Faluda's performance, the bills invited the museum audience (who might not be familiar with drag tipping) into economic exchange by giving them money to tip with. This strategy required the audience to see Faluda's performance *as* labor. She was there to work for her money! Also, the use of global currencies made this labor irrefutably transnational, capturing the global circuits that Faluda's body moves in, that have shaped their precarity as a queer transnational Muslim subject.

I end on the topic of tipping for a few reasons. First, I think Faluda's gimmick is an excellent pedagogical strategy, to teach the audience how to read their body, to place it in a historical and geopolitical frame. As I've discussed, gender is made through reciprocal gestures between audience and witness. But as a performer, how can you give the audience tools to see you and experience your performance on *your* terms? Tipping reminds us that drag is work, it's expensive, and it is an exchange *between* people and places.

Faluda appearing in drag at the museum is the conflu-ence of global movements of bodies, money, politics, and cultural practices, and tipping in international currencies transnationalized, if that's a word, the performance.

Second, introducing tipping into the museum envi-ronment also tipped the scales, it shifted the center of the performance away from reserved high art and toward sexy improvisational play. As audience members offered tips to Faluda, they turned this airy, well-lit, austere, fine arts space—for the duration of one song—into an intimate, seedy, queer club.

Drag doesn't need to look like one thing. Not all drag needs costumes, or makeup, or a stage—drag can be assembled through its bits and pieces and doesn't need a coherent sameness. But to really make a world through performance, through your own body, you *do* have to tip the scale a little, assist the audience over the threshold of imagination so they can witness the trans-formation you're staging, so they can enter the world you're inventing.

Drag is the sum (and sometimes more) of its parts, of technologies (land, architecture, décor, stage, costume, contour, flesh) and techniques (dance, pose, strut, flex, scowl, split). We have so many ways to conjure new worlds through the body! A decolonial approach to drag considers the histories and efficacies of these tools, balancing them to care for minoritarian life and to flaunt irreverence for colonial forms. Go on! Do it!

OUTRODUCTION

Oh hai again!

It's me, LaWhore Vagistan, your favorite over-dressed, over-educated, over-opinionated desi drag aunty! You made it. You read all the words and you reached the other side! I can't believe you missed my show because you were *reading*. But then again, reading is what? Fundamental!

Now it's time to get out of your head, and jump into your body. No Cartesian split for us bitch! No splits at all for me actually, aunty's hamstrings are too tight. You want to decolonize drag? That means doing it.

Try on another version of masculinity.

Wander between androgyny and excess.

Become a monster.

Mess up.

Take a waacking class and pay attention to the new movements it asks of your body.

Stand in front of the mirror for a little longer than you're comfortable.

Get used to other versions of yourself.

Mess up again.

Learn from someone who has done it before.

Pass it on.

Curate a show, and perhaps focus on trans, Indigenous, Black, or Dalit performers.

Pay your performers well and tip them too.

Make room for others, like those who made room for you, your queer, trans, two-spirit mothers, aunties, dads, ancestors, Marshas and Sylvias, divas, icons, crushes, and role models. Like Bob, Peppermint, Shea, Ilona, Kelly, Mercedes, Jackie, Miss Chief, Chanel, Kristi, TT, Gee, Bittu, Papi, Cocoa, Emi, Lemon, Alok, KaMani, Balpreet, Shay, Shu Mai, Khookha, Faluda, Miss Toto, Merrie, Alisha, Vaginal, Casavina, Selena, Delicio, Stormé, Pearl, Mango, Pó, Roxxxy, Violet, Sasha, and Sylvester.

But before you go, perhaps I should warn you: drag *is* transformational. It changes you. It teaches you how others see the everyday version of you. You become self-aware of your body, your gender, your skin, race, posture, hair, feet, and flexibility. You find yourself strangely turned on or off. You find unexpected comforts in high heels and chest binders. Solid colors and symmetrical haircuts become boring. You lose a little hearing from listening to music too loud. Your Uber rating will certainly drop because you're the freak in the back seat.

Drag can be an opening of access to the mess of gender, its possibilities and problems. It allows more people to try on different genders, to refuse them altogether, or make new ones. It is a way of doing gender on your own terms rather than letting gender just happen to you.

The change is incremental—I certainly didn't come to be this stunning overnight. But when you do drag for the stage, 'Gram, TikTok, parade, or nightclub, you allow your body to feel something new. And when you take that body to the street, school, protest, or supermarket it will feel different, because people will act different. Girl, I've seen it. Over this decade of doing drag, I've watched my drag babies grow confidence, radical politics, and even breasts. Drag has been an important venue through which my peers and I have come to understand ourselves as trans and nonbinary and aunty.

It's risky work, but decolonizing drag doesn't get done by reading alone, and it certainly doesn't get done alone. Go. Mess up binaries, borders, and history. Make a beautiful fucking mess.

RuPaul tells the queens on every episode of *Drag Race*, "Don't fuck it up!"

I'm here to tell you to: FUCK. IT. UP.

Ex. Oh. Ex.
—Aunty

ACKNOWLEDGMENTS

Major gay thanks go to my colleagues Mac Irvine, Manjari Mukherjee, Wenxuan Xue, Lilian Mengesha, AB Brown, and Christine Mok for their feedback on this manuscript. Especially queer thanks to Bhakti Shringarpure for her generosity and patience as editor. Also, sugar baby gratitude to the Tufts University Faculty Research Awards Committee and the New England Humanities Consortium for the funding they provided toward completing this research. May the drag goddesses shower their blessings on all my friends (and sometimes strangers) who I have dragged to shows with me over the years. Glitter and sparkles for the performers in the book and beyond, whose embodied brilliance keep me returning to the nightclub despite my increasingly early bedtime. Bubbles and rainbows for the students in my Critical Drag undergraduate classes who helped me experiment with combining critique and pleasure. And last, effusive love to my families, bio and chosen, who have given me room to be my draggiest self.

Drag artists are the future! Tip them well, and let them lead the way.

NOTES

1   David Román, "Dance Liberation," *Theatre Journal* 55, no. 3 (2003).

2   "Historic Drag Show Draws Hundreds to Navajo Nation, Funds Raised for LGBTQ+ Scholarship," *Navajo Nation Pride* 2019, https://www.navajonationpride.com/post/historic-drag-show-draws-hundreds-to-navajo-nation-funds-raised-for-lgbtq-scholarship.

3   Kareem Khubchandani, *Ishtyle: Accenting Gay Indian Nightlife* (Ann Arbor: University of Michigan Press, 2020).

4   Sarah Moon and Hollie Silverman, "A California Fire Sparked by a Gender Reveal Party Has Grown to More Than 10,000 Acres," *CNN*, September 8, 2020, https://www.cnn.com/2020/09/08/us/el-dorado-fire-gender-reveal-update-trnd/index.html.

5   Iain Morland, "Intersex," *TSQ: Transgender Studies Quarterly* 1, no. 1-2 (2014).

6   Thomas Laqueur, *Making Sex: Body and Gender from the Greeks to Freud* (Harvard University Press, 1992); Karen Harvey, "The Century of Sex? Gender, Bodies, and Sexuality in the Long Eighteenth Century," *The Historical Journal* 45, no. 4 (2002).

7   Jules Gill-Peterson, *Histories of the Transgender Child* (Minneapolis: University of Minnesota Press, 2018).

8   Omise'eke Natasha Tinsley, *Ezili's Mirrors: Imagining Black Queer Genders* (Durham: Duke University Press, 2018), 58.

9   C. Riley Snorton, "'A New Hope': The Psychic Life of Passing," *Hypatia* 24, no. 3 (2009).

10   Jane Ward, "Gender Labor: Transmen, Femmes, and Collective Work of Transgression," *Sexualities* 13, no. 2 (2010).

11   Marlon M. Bailey, *Butch Queens up in Pumps: Gender, Performance, and Ballroom Culture in Detroit* (Ann Arbor: University of Michigan, 2013).

12   Amrou Al-Kadhi, *Unicorn: The Memoir of a Muslim Drag Queen* (London: Fourth Estate, 2019).

13   Judith Butler, *Gender Trouble: Feminism and the Subversion of Identity* (New York: Routledge, 2006).

14   Eve Kosofsky Sedgwick, "Gosh, Boy George, You Must Be Awfully Secure in Your Masculinity!," in *Constructing Masculinity*, eds. Brian Wallis, Maurice Berger, and Simon Watson (New York: Routledge, 1995).

15   Ibid. 16.

16   Meredith Heller, *Queering Drag: Redefining the Discourse of Gender-Bending* (Bloomington: Indiana University Press, 2020), 180.

17   Butler, *Gender Trouble,* 190; Hortense J. Spillers, "Mama's Baby, Papa's Maybe: An American Grammar Book," *Diacritics* 17, no. 2 (1987).

18   Sam Feder, "Disclosure: Trans Lives on Screen," (Field of Vision, 2020).

19   "Balpreet Kaur, Sikh Woman, Receives Remarkable Apology from Redditor Who Posted Her Photo," *Huffpost* 2012. https://www.huffpost.com/entry/balpreet-kaur-receives-recieves-remarkable-apology-from-redditor_n_1919336.

20   I also want to acknowledge there is also public discourse around body hair being understood as traces of colonialism, and in particular colonial rape and the impinging of white genetics on Indigenous people. What counts as a decolonial aesthetic is never cut and dry.

21   Anne E. Butler, "Khookha Mcqueer (1987–)," in *Global Encyclopedia of Lesbian, Gay, Bisexual, Transgender, and Queer*

History, ed. Howard Chiang, et al. (Farmington Hills, MI: Charles Scribner's Sons, 2019).

22   George Chauncey, *Gay New York: Gender, Urban Culture, and the Makings of the Gay Male World, 1890-1940* (New York: Basic Books, 1994); Michelle Liu Carriger, "'The Unnatural History and Petticoat Mystery of Boulton and Park': A Victorian Sex Scandal and the Theatre Defense," *TDR : The Drama Review* 57, no. 4 (2013).

23   Gail Bederman, *Manliness & Civilization: A Cultural History of Gender and Race in the United States, 1880-1917* (Chicago: University of Chicago Press, 1995); Mrinalini Sinha, *Colonial Masculinity: The 'Manly Englishman' and the' Effeminate Bengali' in the Late Nineteenth Century* (Manchester: Manchester University Press, 1995); Scott Morgensen, "Settler Homonationalism: Theorizing Settler Colonialism within Queer Modernities," *GLQ* 16, no. 1-2 (2010); Jasbir K. Puar, *Terrorist Assemblages: Homonationalism in Queer Times* (Durham: Duke University Press, 2007).

24   Emma Tarlo, *Clothing Matters: Dress and Identity in India* (Chicago, IL: University of Chicago Press, 1996).

25   Andrew Bank, "Of 'Native Skulls' and 'Noble Caucasians': Phrenology in Colonial South Africa," *Journal of Southern African Studies* 22, no. 3 (1996).

26   Siobhan B. Somerville, *Queering the Color Line: Race and the Invention of Homosexuality in American Culture* (Durham, NC: Duke University Press, 2000).

27   Jasbir Puar and Amit Rai, "Monster, Terrorist, Fag: The War on Terrorism and the Production of Docile Patriots," *Social Text* 20, no. 3 (2002).

28   Puar, *Terrorist Assemblages,* and Ryan Ashley Caldwell, *Fallgirls: Gender and the Framing of Torture at Abu Ghraib* (Burlington, VT: Ashgate, 2012).

29   Morgensen, "Settler Homonationalism."

30   Spillers, "Mama's Baby, Papa's Maybe."

31   C. Riley Snorton, *Black on Both Sides: A Racial History of Trans Identity* (Minneapolis: University of Minnesota Press, 2017); Tinsley, *Ezili's Mirrors*.

32   Manan Desai, "Korla Pandit Plays America: Exotica, Racial Performance, and Fantasies of Containment in Cold War Culture," *The Journal of Popular Culture* 48, no. 4 (2015); Sean Metzger, *Chinese Looks: Fashion, Performance, Race* (Bloomington: Indiana University Press, 2014).

33   Jessica Hinchy, *Governing Gender and Sexuality in Colonial India: The Hijra, C. 1850-1900* (Cambridge: Cambridge University Press, 2019); Anjali R. Arondekar, *For the Record: On Sexuality and the Colonial Archive in India* (Durham: Duke University Press, 2009); Arvind Narrain and Alok Gupta, *Law Like Love: Queer Perspectives on Law*, Sexualities (New Delhi: Yoda Press, 2011).

34   Kareem Khubchandani, "Staging Transgender Solidarities at Bangalore's Queer Pride," *Transgender Studies Quarterly* 1, no. 4 (2014).

35   Ballroom culture is now a global phenomenon, and while its roots are placed in Harlem in the 1970s, many Black social and leisure events described as balls and featuring gender-nonconforming performance existed across the US since the late nineteenth century. I'm drawing here on Marlon Bailey's research on Ball culture in Detroit, where the circulation of New York City's particular brand of nightlife, staged and circulated in the documentary *Paris Is Burning* (Jennie Livingston, 1990), suture to Detroit's historical Black queer and trans ball cultures.

36   Bailey, *Butch Queens up in Pumps*, 36.

37   Dredge Byung'Chu Käng, "Idols of Development: Transnational Transgender Performance in Thai K-Pop Cover Dance," *Transgender Studies Quarterly* 1, no. 4 (2014).

38   Morgensen, "Settler Homonationalism."

39   "Dance to the Berdash," Smithsonian American Art Museum, https://www.si.edu/object/dance-berdash:saam_1985.66.442.

40 Stefan Zebrowski-Rubin, "Dance of Two Spirits–Kent Monkman at Montreal's Museum of Fine Arts," *artblog,* August 18, 2009, https://www.theartblog.org/2009/08/dance-of-two-spirits-kent-monkman-at-montreals-museum-of-fine-arts/.

41 Joshua Trey Barnett and Corey W. Johnson, "We Are All Royalty," *Journal of Leisure Research* 45, no. 5 (2017). 678.

42 J. Halberstam, *Female Masculinity* (Durham: Duke University Press, 1998); Marcia Ochoa, *Queen for a Day: Transformistas, Beauty Queens, and the Performance of Femininity in Venezuela* (Durham; London: Duke University Press, 2014).

43 Kareem Khubchandani, "Snakes on the Dance Floor: Bollywood, Gesture, and Gender," *The Velvet Light Trap* no. 77, Spring (2016).

44 Sarah Hankins, "'I'm a Cross between a Clown, a Stripper, and a Streetwalker': Drag Tipping, Sex Work, and a Queer Sociosexual Economy," *Signs: Journal of Women in Culture and Society* 40, no. 2 (2015).

45 We can think widely with alternative forms of desire such as communities of Furries and people who desire or are in relationships with objects such as cars and monuments. But as Amber Musser has beautifully argued, even objectum sexuals, people who desire objects, often gender them as masculine or feminine as a way of making their unruly desire more socially acceptable. Amber Musser, "Objects of Desire: Toward an Ethics of Sameness," *Theory & Event* 16, no. 2 (2013).

46 Verta Taylor and Leila J. Rupp, "Learning from Drag Queens," *Contexts* 5, no. 3 (2006); Justine Egner and Patricia Maloney, "'It Has No Color, It Has No Gender, It's Gender Bending': Gender and Sexuality Fluidity and Subversiveness in Drag Performance," *Journal of Homosexuality* 63, no. 7 (2015).

47 Benjamin Hegarty, "Under the Lights, onto the Stage," *Transgender Studies Quarterly* 5, no. 3 (2018). 360.

48 Jason Patton and Stacee Reicherzer, "Transsexual Drag Entertainers as Keepers of Queer Power-Knowledge," *The Electronic Journal of Human Sexuality* 15 (2012).

49 Ibid.

50 Deborah Parédez, *Selenidad: Selena, Latinos, and the Performance of Memory* (Durham NC: Duke University Press, 2009), 181.

51 Ibid., 184.

52 Karen Shimakawa, *National Abjection: The Asian American Body Onstage* (Durham: Duke UP, 2002); José Esteban Muñoz, *Disidentifications: Queers of Color and the Performance of Politics* (Minneapolis: University of Minnesota Press, 1999).

53 Eng-Beng Lim, *Brown Boys and Rice Queens: Spellbinding Performance in the Asias* (New York: New York University, 2013).

54 Tarlo, *Clothing Matters*; Lim, *Brown Boys and Rice Queens*.

55 C. Winter Han, *Geisha of a Different Kind: Race and Sexuality in Gaysian America* (New York: New York University Press, 2015).

56 Ibid.

57 J. Halberstam, "Mackdaddy, Superfly, Rapper: Gender, Race, and Masculinity in the Drag King Scene," *Social Text* no. 52/53 (1997).

58 Ibid.

59 Malik Gaines, *Black Performance on the Outskirts of the Left: A History of the Impossible* (New York: New York University, 2017).

60 Ibid., 141.

61 Bailey, *Butch Queens Up in Pumps*, 59. Emphasis mine.

62 Ibid.

63 Ibid., 68.

64 Bryce Lease, "Realness & The Digital Archive: South African Drag Online," *Contemporary Theatre Review* 31, no. 1-2 (2021).

65 Lynda Johnston, "Sites of Excess: The Spatial Politics of Touch for Drag Queens in Aotearoa New Zealand," *Emotion, Space and Society* 5, no. 1 (2012).

66 Kalissa Alexeyeff, "Globalizing Drag in the Cook Islands: Friction, Repulsion, and Abjection," *The Contemporary Pacific* 20, no. 1 (2008): 150.

67 Ibid., 154.

68   Jasbir K. Puar, "Global Circuits: Transnational Sexualities and
      Trinidad," *Signs: Journal of Women in Culture and Society* 26, no. 1
      (2001): 1055.

69   Edward Ndopu and Darnell L. Moore, "On Ableism Within
      Queer Spaces, or, Queering the 'Normal'," We'll All Be Ancients,
      2013, https://wellallbeancients.tumblr.com/post/46895332103/
      on-ableism-within-queer-spaces-or-queering-the; Caleb Luna,
      "The Gender Nonconformity of My Fatness," The Body is
      not an Apology, 2018, https://thebodyisnotanapology.com/
      magazine/the-gender-nonconformity-of-my-fatness/; Ellen
      Samuels, "My Body, My Closet: Invisible Disability and the
      Limits of Coming-out Discourse," *GLQ* 9, no. 1-2 (2003).

70   Jennifer Spruill, "Ad/Dressing the Nation: Drag and
      Authenticity in Post-Apartheid South Africa," *Journal of
      Homosexuality* 46, no. 3-4 (2004).

71   Lee-Ann Olwage and Sasha Ingber, "PHOTOS: Drag
      Queens in South Africa Embrace Queerness and Tradition,"
      NPR, September 20, 2019, https://www.npr.org/sections/
      goatsandsoda/2019/09/20/761990035/photos-drag-queens-in-
      south-africa-embrace-queerness-and-tradition.

72   Madison Moore, *Fabulous: The Rise of the Beautiful Eccentric*
      (New Haven: Yale University Press, 2018); Brian A. Horton,
      "Fashioning Fabulation: Dress, Gesture and the Queer Aesthetics
      of Mumbai Pride," *South Asia* 43, no. 2 (2020).

73   Kareem Khubchandani, "Between Screens and Bodies: New Queer
      Performance in India," in *Pop Empires: Transnational and Diasporic
      Flows of India and Korea*, eds. Robert Ji-Song Ku, S. Heijin Lee, and
      Monika Mehta (Honolulu: University of Hawaii Press, 2019).

74   Elizabeth Kaminski and Verta Taylor, "We're Not Just
      Lip-Synching up Here: Music and Collective Identity in Drag
      Performances," in *Identity Work in Social Movements*, ed. Jo Reger
      et al. (University of Minnesota Press, 2008), 51.

75   Jeff Roy, "Translating Hijra into Transgender: Performance and
      Pehchān in India's Trans-Hijra Communities," *Transgender Studies
      Quarterly* 3, no. 3-4 (2016).

76   Naomi Bragin, "Techniques of Black Male Re/Dress: Corporeal
     Drag and Kinesthetic Politics in the Rebirth of Waacking/
     Punkin'," *Women & Performance: a journal of feminist theory* 24,
     no. 1 (2014).

77   Elspeth H. Brown, *Work: A Queer History of Modeling* (Durham:
     Duke University Press, 2019).

78   Thomas F. DeFrantz, "Bone-Breaking, Black Social Dance, and
     Queer Corporeal Orature," *The Black Scholar* 46, no. 1 (2016).

79   Anna Martine Whitehead, "Expressing Life through Loss: On
     Queens That Fall with a Freak Technique," in *Queer Dance:
     Meanings and Makings*, ed. Clare Croft (New York, NY: Oxford
     University Press, 2017).

80   Jared Mackley-Crump and Kirsten Zemke, "'Sissy That Walk':
     Reframing queer Pacific bodies through the FAFSWAG Ball,"
     Queer Studies in Media and Popular Culture 4, no. 1 (2019).

81   Gayatri Reddy, *With Respect to Sex: Negotiating Hijra Identity in
     South India* (Chicago: University of Chicago Press, 2005).

82   David Valentine, *Imagining Transgender: An Ethnography of a
     Category* (Durham: Duke University Press, 2007).

83   Robert Diaz, "Queer Unsettlements: Diasporic Filipinos in
     Canada's World Pride," *Journal of Asian American studies* 19, no. 3
     (2016).

84   Cole Rizki, "Latin/X American Trans Studies: Toward a Travesti-
     Trans Analytic," *Transgender Studies Quarterly* 6, no. 2 (2019).

85   Selby Wynn Schwartz, The Bodies of Others : Drag Dances and
     Their Afterlives, (Ann Arbor: University of Michigan Press,, 2019).

86   Kevin Gotkin, "Crip Club Vibes: Technologies for New
     Nightlife," *Catalyst: Feminism, Theory, Technoscience* 5, no. 1 (2019).

87   Zachary Zane, "Meet Deafies in Drag: Youtube's Deaf, Latino
     Comedy Duo," *Out*, May 25, 2017, https://www.out.com/
     popnography/2017/5/25/meet-deafies-drag-youtubes-deaf-
     latino-comedy-duo.

88   Arti Sandhu, "India's Digital Drag Aunties: Breaking New
     Ground Wearing Familiar Fashions," *Dress: Special Issue:
     LGBTQ+ Fashions, Styles, and Bodies* 45, no. 1 (2019). Disemelo

Katlego, "Performing the Queer Archive: Strategies of Self-Styling on Instagram," *Acts of Transgression* eds. Jay Pather and Catherin Boulle (Johannesburg: Wits University Press, 2019), 219–242.

89 Sue-Ellen Case, "Towards a Butch-Femme Aesthetic," *Discourse* 11, no. 1 (1988).

90 Susan Stryker, "Cross-Dressing for Empire: Race, Class, and Gender Performance at the Bohemian Grove." Unpublished paper.

91 Clare Sears, "All That Glitters: Trans-Ing California's Gold Rush Migrations," *GLQ* 14, no. 2–3 (2008).

92 Käng, "Idols of Development," 563.

93 Harshita Mruthinti Kamath, *Impersonations: The Artifice of Brahmin Masculinity in South Indian Dance* (Oakland: University of California Press, 2019).

94 Amanda Lock Swarr, "Moffies, Artists, and Queens: Race and the Production of South African Gay Male Drag," *Journal of Homosexuality* 46, no. 3–4 (2004): 78.

95 Michael Schulman, "In Drag, It Turns out, There Are Second Acts," *The New York Times* 2014, https://www.nytimes.com/2014/02/23/fashion/RuPaul-Drag-Race-television.html; Evan Ross Katz, "Race to the Top: 10 Years of RuPaul," *Paper* 2019, https://www.papermag.com/the-decade-in-rupaul-2641948905.html.

96 Even though she primarily makes public appearances in her masculine persona, I use feminine pronouns for RuPaul as I know her best in her drag queen incarnation on the TV screen.

97 Manuel Betancourt, "The Rise of RuPaul's Drag Industrial Complex," *Vice* 2017, https://www.vice.com/en/article/3dmpdw/the-rise-of-rupauls-drag-industrial-complex; Jimmy Im, "How 'RuPaul's Drag Race' Helped Mainstream Drag Culture — and Spawned a Brand Bringing in Millions," *CNBC*, 2019, https://www.cnbc.com/2018/09/28/rupauls-drag-race-inspired-multimillion-dollar-conference-dragcon.html.

 98   Abby Aguirre, "How the World Fell Head over Heels for
      RuPaul," *Vogue* 2019, https://www.vogue.com/article/rupaul-
      interview-may-2019-issue.

 99   Ibid.; Jenna Wortham, "Is 'RuPaul's Drag Race' the Most
      Radical Show on TV?," *The New York Times* 2018, https://
      www.nytimes.com/2018/01/24/magazine/is-rupauls-drag-
      race-the-most-radical-show-on-tv.html.

100   Aguirre, "How the World . . . "; Meredith Blake, "RuPaul
      Has 'Done Everything.' Except This," *Los Angeles Times*
      2020, https://www.latimes.com/entertainment-arts/tv/
      story/2020-01-02/rupaul-netflix-aj-and-the-queen-drag-
      race; J Davenport, "From the Love Ball to RuPaul: The
      Mainstreaming of Drag in the 1990s," (ProQuest Dissertations
      Publishing, 2017); Richard Lawson, "The Philosopher
      Queen," *Vanity Fair* 2020, https://archive.vanityfair.com/
      article/2020/1/the-philosopher-queen; Schulman, "In Drag, It
      Turns out . . . "

101   Davenport, "From the Love Ball to RuPaul," 145.

102   Lawson, "The Philosopher Queen."

103   Davenport, "From the Love Ball to RuPaul," 168.

104   Decca Aitkenhead, "RuPaul: 'Drag Is a Big F-You to Male-
      Dominated Culture'," *The Guardian* 2018, https://www.
      theguardian.com/tv-and-radio/2018/mar/03/rupaul-drag-
      race-big-f-you-to-male-dominated-culture.

105   TFL, "From Ad Revenues to Multi-Million Dollar Events:
      The Big Business That Is RuPaul's Drag Race," *The
      Fashion Law* 2019, https://www.thefashionlaw.com/the-
      big-business-that-is-rupauls-drag-race/; Lawson, "The
      Philosopher Queen."

106   TFL, "From Ad Revenues . . . "

107   Alyxandra Vesey, "'A Way to Sell Your Records': Pop Stardom
      and the Politics of Drag Professionalization on RuPaul's Drag
      Race," *Television & New Media* 18, no. 7 (2017).

108   Carl Douglas Schottmiller, "Reading RuPaul's Drag Race:
      Queer Memory, Camp Capitalism, and Rupaul's Drag Empire,"
      (ProQuest Dissertations Publishing, 2017).

109 Ruth Reader, "Cash Is Queen: As Tweens Flock to 'RuPaul's Drag Race,' Retailers Follow," *Fast Company* 2018, https://www.fastcompany.com/40532164/cash-is-queen-as-tweens-flock-to-rupauls-drag-race-retailers-follow.

110 Leo Duran, "When Drag Queens Promote It, Fans Will Buy It," *Marketplace* 2018, https://www.marketplace.org/2018/07/03/business/they-honestly-start-trends-and-other-reasons-why-drag-queens-fans-are-spending/.

111 Danielle Chiriguayo and Janet Nguyen, "A Tale of Two Cities: How Drag Performers in Los Angeles and Moscow, Idaho, Spend Their Money," *Marketplace* 2018, https://www.marketplace.org/2018/10/23/drag-queens-and-drag-kings-two-different-cities-2/.

112 Schulman, "In Drag, It Turns out . . . "

113 Lawson, "The Philosopher Queen."

114 Isaac Oliver, "Is This the Golden Age of Drag? Yes. And No.," *The New York Times* 2018, https://www.nytimes.com/2018/01/17/arts/drag-queens-rupaul-drag-race.html.

115 Ash Percival, "RuPaul's Drag Race Star Silky Ganache Calls for Better Contestant Aftercare: 'Is It Going to Take a Queen to Kill Herself?'," *Huffpost* 2019, https://www.huffingtonpost.co.uk/entry/rupauls-drag-race-aftercare-silky-nutmeg-ganache_uk_5d7388fae4b06451356e7bb1.

116 Oliver, "Is This the Golden Age of Drag?"

117 Frantz Fanon, *Black Skin, White Masks* (New York: Grove, 2008).

118 Megan Goodwin and Ilyse Morgenstein Fuerst, *Ru-Ligion Ru-Vealed - the T on Religion & Drag Race*, podcast audio, *Keeping it 101* 2020, https://keepingit101.com/e108.

119 Schottmiller, "Reading RuPaul's Drag Race," 208-10.

120 Ibid., 218.

121 Ibid., 234.

122 Lauren Aratani, "Did RuPaul Just Announce He Has a Fracking Empire on His Ranch?," *The Guardian* 2020, https://www.theguardian.com/tv-and-radio/2020/mar/21/rupaul-fracking-wyoming-ranch-land-oil.

123 Oliver, "Is This the Golden Age of Drag?"

124   Puar, *Terrorist Assemblages*; Megan Goodwin and Ilyse Fuerst
        Morgenstein, "How a Stars and Stripes Hijab on 'RuPaul's
        Drag Race' Reveals America's Troubling Relationship to
        Gender, Ethnicity and 'That' Religion," *Religion Dispatches*
        2020, https://religiondispatches.org/how-a-stars-and-stripes-
        hijab-on-rupauls-drag-race-reveals-americas-troubling-
        relationship-to-gender-ethnicity-and-that-religion/.

125   For an extended conversation about Cox on *Drag Race* see:
        Talib Jabbar, "Drag Queens in Stars and Stripes," *Post45* 2022,
        https://post45.org/2022/12/drag-queens-in-stars-and-stripes/.

126   Niall Brennan and David Gudelunas, *RuPaul's Drag Race and
        the Shifting Visibility of Drag Culture: The Boundaries of Reality TV*
        (Cham: Springer International Publishing AG, 2017).

127   Matthew Goldmark, "National Drag: The Language of
        Inclusion in RuPaul's Drag Race," *GLQ* 21, no. 4 (2015).

128   E. Zhang, "Memoirs of a Gay! Sha: Race and Gender
        Performance on RuPaul's Drag Race," *Studies in Costume &
        Performance* 1, no. 1 (2016).

129   Spencer Kornhaber, "The Fierceness of 'Femme, Fat,
        and Asian'," *The Atlantic* 2016, https://www.theatlantic.
        com/entertainment/archive/2016/05/kim-chi-rupauls-
        drag-race-femme-fat-asian-c-winter-han-interview-
        middlebury/483527/.

130   Jason Ritchie, "How Do You Say 'Come out of the Closet' in
        Arabic?: Queer Activism and the Politics of Visibility in Israel-
        Palestine," *GLQ* 16, no. 4 (2010).

131   Sabrina Strings and Long T. Bui, "'She Is Not Acting, She Is':
        The Conflict between Gender and Racial Realness on RuPaul's
        Drag Race," *Feminist Media Studies* 14, no. 5 (2014): 827.

132   Ibid., 828.

133   Nishant Upadhyay, "'Can You Get More American Than
        Native American?': Drag and Settler Colonialism in RuPaul's
        Drag Race," *Cultural Studies: Cultural Production under Multiple
        Colonialisms* 33, no. 3 (2019): 493.

134   Ibid; Morgensen, "Settler Homonationalism"; Andrea Smith,
      "Queer Theory and Native Studies," *GLQ* 2010 Vol. 16, Issue
      1–2.

135   Senthorun Raj, "A/Effective Adjudications: Queer Refugees
      and the Law," *Journal of intercultural studies* 38, no. 4 (2017).

136   Rinaldo Walcott, *Queer Returns: Essays on Multiculturalism,
      Diaspora, and Black Studies* (London, Ontario, Canada:
      Insomniac Press, 2016).

137   Maija Kappler, "Ilona Verley Is 1st 'Canada's Drag Race'
      Contestant to Get the Vogue Treatment," *HuffPost* 2020,
      https://www.huffingtonpost.ca/entry/canada-drag-race-ilona-
      verley-vogue_ca_5f5134a0c5b6578026cb1e81.

138   Jonathan Ore, "America's First Drag Queen Was a Former
      Slave and LGBT Rights Crusader, Says Historian," *CBC
      Radio* 2020, https://www.cbc.ca/radio/day6/teck-frontier-
      mine-medical-assistance-in-dying-1990s-mls-wilson-cruz-
      the-first-drag-queen-and-more-1.5477892/america-s-first-
      drag-queen-was-a-former-slave-and-lgbt-rights-crusader-says-
      historian-1.5478181.

139   Shaka McGlotten, *Dragging: Or, in the Drag of a Queer Life*,
      (New York, NY: Routledge, 2019). 73–77.

140   Juana. M. Rodriguez, "Queer Sociality and Other Sexual
      Fantasies," *GLQ* 17, no. 2–3 (2011).

141   Patrick Wolfe, *Settler Colonialism and the Transformation of
      Anthropology: The Politics and Poetics of an Ethnographic Event*
      (New York: Cassell, 1999).

142   Stephanie N. Teves, *Defiant Indigeneity: The Politics of Hawaiian
      Performance* (Chapel Hill: The University of North Carolina
      Press, 2018).

143   Ibid., 107.

144   Adria L. Imada, *Aloha America: Hula Circuits through the U.S.
      Empire* (Durham: Duke University Press, 2012).

145   Michael Moon, "Flaming Closets," *October* Vol. 51, Winter
      (1989).

146   Sofia Vranou, "'Pakis from Outer Space': Oriental
      Postmodernity in Leigh Bowery's Performative Costuming,"
      Studies in Costume & Performance 5 (2020).

147   Gayatri Gopinath, *Impossible Desires: Queer Diasporas and
      South Asian Public Cultures* (Durham: Duke University Press,
      2005), 29.

148   RiceRockettes, "Chi-Chi Kago – Shanti/Ashtangi – Die
      Another Day (Drag Queen Parody)," *YouTube* 2014, https://
      www.youtube.com/watch?v=cerXHtVm2gI.

149   Monisha Das Gupta, *Unruly Immigrants: Rights, Activism, and
      Transnational South Asian Politics in the United States* (Durham:
      Duke University Press, 2006).

150   Shu Mai's performance track draws on new trends in drag
      performance. Editing software that allows you to effortlessly rip
      sound from the video has made lip-synching to spoken word
      (as opposed to song) easier to do. Also, the ability to easily
      record and layer tracks on one's home computer allows drag
      performers to sing (sometimes quite badly) their own parodies
      for shows.

151   Ruth Wilson Gilmore, *Golden Gulag: Prisons, Surplus, Crisis,
      and Opposition in Globalizing California* (Berkeley: University of
      California Press, 2007); Regina G. Kunzel, *Criminal Intimacy:
      Prison and the Uneven History of Modern American Sexuality*
      (Chicago: University of Chicago Press, 2008).

152   Khubchandani, "Staging Transgender Solidarities . . ."

153   "Peach Paradise" (Dir. Shiva Raichandani), 2022.

154   Vivian L. Huang, "Sparking Joy, Serving Mess: The Drag of
      Asian/American History," *Journal of popular culture* 53, no. 6
      (2020).

155   It is telling that the white stagehand in the YouTube recording
      of this performance gets distracted and forgets to bring the
      final wig to Merrie, and when she does she puts on the wrong
      one. Even in post-slavery contexts, white people cannot bring
      themselves to wait on Black folks.

156 Nayan Shah, *Contagious Divides: Epidemics and Race in San Francisco's Chinatown* (Berkeley: University of California Press, 2001).

157 Joe Parslow, "Not Another Drag Competition: From Amateur to Professional Drag Performance," *Performance research* 25, no. 1 (2020).

158 Muñoz, *Disidentifications.*

159 Melissa M. Wilcox, *Queer Nuns: Religion, Activism, and Serious Parody*, vol. 33 (New York: New York University Press, 2018), 20.

160 K. Bradford, "Grease Cowboy Fever or, the Making of Johnny T," *Journal of homosexuality* 43, no. 3-4 (2003): 16.

161 Schlueter Jennifer, "'How You Durrin?': Chuck Knipp, Shirley Q. Liquor, and Contemporary Blackface," *TDR : Drama review* 57, no. 2 (2013).

162 Shane T. Moreman and Dawn Marie McIntosh, "Brown Scriptings and Rescriptings: A Critical Performance Ethnography of Latina Drag Queens," *Communication and Critical/Cultural Studies* 7, no. 2 (2010): 124.

163 Andrew Farrell, "Lipstick Clapsticks: A Yarn and a Kiki with an Aboriginal Drag Queen," *AlterNative: an international journal of indigenous peoples* 12, no. 5 (2016): 575.

164 Spruill, "Ad/Dressing the Nation"; Sandhu, "India's Digital Drag Aunties: Breaking New Ground Wearing Familiar Fashions," 56.

165 Spruill, "Ad/Dressing the Nation," 95.

166 Teves, *Defiant Indigeneity*, 95.

167 Ibid.

168 Deborah R. Vargas, "Rita's Pants: The Charro Traje and Trans-Sensuality," *Women & performance* 20, no. 1 (2010).

169 Ibid.; Hankins, "I'm a Cross between a Clown . . . "

170 Lucy Mae San Pablo Burns, "'Your Terno's Draggin': Fashioning Filipino American Performance," *Women & performance* 21, no. 2 (2011); Michelle Liu Carriger, "No 'Thing

to Wear': A Brief History of Kimono and Inappropriation from Japonisme to Kimono Protests," *Theatre research international* 43, no. 2 (2018); Elizabeth R Escobedo, *From Coveralls to Zoot Suits: The Lives of Mexican American Women on the World War Ii Home Front* (Chapel Hill: University of North Carolina Press, 2013).

171   E. Patrick Johnson, "'Scatter the Pigeons': Baldness and the Performance of Black Hypermasculinity," in *Blackberries and Redbones: Critical Articulations of Black Hair/Body Politics in Africana Communities*, eds. Regina E. Spellers and Kimberly R. Moffitt (Cresskill: Hampton Press, 2010).

172   Egner and Maloney, "'It Has No Color . . . '" 881.

173   Ramón H. Rivera-Servera, "Anti-Drag Choreographies and the Trans Aesthetics of Pó Rodil," presented at *Drag Kings: An Archeology of Spectacular Masculinities in Latino America symposium* (Princeton University, 2019).

174   Heller, *Queering Drag,* 118.

175   Esther Newton, *Mother Camp: Female Impersonators in America*, (Chicago: University of Chicago Press, 1979).

176   M. Leslie Santana, "Una Peña En Párraga: Drag Kings and Cuba's Sexual Revolution," in *Queer Nightlife*, eds. Kemi Adeyemi, Kareem Khubchandani, and Ramón H. Rivera-Servera (Ann Arbor: University of Michigan Press, 2021).

177   Mary L. Gray, *Out in the country: youth, media, and queer visibility in rural America* (New York: New York University Press 2009).

178   Hankins, "I'm a Cross between a Clown . . . "

KAREEM KHUBCHANDANI is an Associate Professor at Tufts University. He is the author of the award winning *Ishtyle: Accenting Gay Indian Nightlife*, co-editor of the Lambda Literary-nominated *Queer Nightlife*, and curator of Critical Aunty Studies. He also performs as LaWhore Vagistan, everyone's favorite South Asian drag aunty.